Nest Amongst Temples

My travels in India

By

Jillain McKay

2014

Nestled Amongst Temples © 2014 Jillain McKay
Triplicity Publishing, LLC

ISBN-13: 978-0990813354
ISBN-10: 0990813355

First Edition – 2014
Cover Design: Nancy McCarthy
Interior Design: Triplicity Publishing, LLC
Editor: Christy Dyer - Triplicity Publishing, LLC

For Otis George whose smile outshines every sunbeam.

The little red house by the dirt track road
is the perfect place to be,
It's quirky and quaint with its faded red paint
just right for the Noodle and me.

Nestled amongst temples, guarded by Gods,
the Noodle and I will be fine,
Busy at markets then counting our cash
t'is the start of the MamaNoo line.

(Text message sent to Nancy on receiving a picture of the
house from her, prior to my travels)

Contents

Chapter 1: New Horizons

The palm trees lazily wave at me as I ride along the pot-holed road from Anjuna to Mapsa. Ahead, my beautiful daughter, Nancy, is sitting ramrod straight on her scooter, her long dark curls, shiny in the sunlight, are dancing with the breeze. She looks a picture of elegance as she rides along; a Tuesday's child, full of grace. Every so often she stops at a junction to allow me to catch up with her. I ride slowly, very slowly, so much that it has become a joke that even the cows wandering along the roads overtake me. Unlike my daughter, I do not appear a picture of elegance. My knuckles are white from tension as I grip the handlebars of the scooter; I frown in concentration at the road ahead, barely daring to glance at the beautiful scenery all around. My shoulders and neck are stiff and every so often I have to wiggle my head and shrug my shoulders in an effort to relax.

"Are you all right, Mama?" Nancy calls out to me as I drive closer to where she has stopped, once again, for me to catch up with her.

"Yes, I'm fine really, darling, it's just a matter of gaining my confidence. I'll be ok, don't worry. It's just that I haven't a clue where I am and I'm a bit scared of losing you."

"Don't worry about losing me, there are road signs you can follow."

1

"Darling, I daren't take my eyes off the road to look for signs. The drivers are crazy, there are animals wandering onto the road and everybody seems to be blasting their horns at me, I'm terrified."

"Don't worry, I'll go slowly, you'll get used to it."

I wish I had my daughter's confidence at this point. I have been riding the scooter for almost a week now and I am still scared witless every time I get on it, which I will only do if I am following her. Five weeks into this adventure and I am feeling rather vulnerable, certainly not something I had envisaged a year earlier when I had agreed to the trip.

*

The previous year had been my annus horribilis. I was engaged to be married but the relationship was broken off and although I had no doubts that this was the right thing to do, it still resulted in much heartbreak and soul searching. Shortly after this, my beloved horse, Simon, whom I had owned since he was 11, had to be put down at the age of 30. It was expected, but still an awful blow, not least witnessing the felling of such a huge creature — pitiful and haunting. Some weeks following this incident, my constant canine companion, Miss Bridget, a gorgeous little Boxer dog, was diagnosed with a virulent cancer in her ear and also had to be put to sleep. It was almost more than I could bear. Nancy, hearing of my latest tragedy, phoned me from Mumbai, India, where she was working as a textile designer for an Indian company. We discussed the episodes of the last year and she expressed her sorrow and then said something that rang a bell in my head, the echoes of which stayed with me long after the phone call.

"It does seem that the way is being cleared for you to do something, Mama. Look, all of your responsibilities are disappearing at once."

It was true, it had been a long time since I could just up and go away for a weekend or holiday without the encumbrance of making arrangements for children or animals to be looked after. That evening I booked a weekend retreat away.

It wasn't long after this phone call that Nancy called again with a proposition.

"I've been thinking about starting my own design company. I think I could do it, it's possible in India and I've learnt so much since I've been out here."

"What would you design, darling?"

"I was thinking handbags. I've found out where Gucci source their leather in Mumbai and I've got friends who can show me the area. I think it's now or never and I've always wanted to run my own business. I'll get the bags made up in Mumbai, but live in Goa and sell the bags on the markets. I can do this for a season and see how it goes; see whether my designs will sell. I can get an overnight bus to Mumbai and back when I need more bags, and I've got friends in Mumbai who I can stay with. My contract here ends in a year's time and I reckon I can save up enough money to last me though another six months in India, as long as I'm careful."

"Well, why not? You've got nothing to lose, if it works out, great and, if not, then you've had six months in Goa, which is lovely. Don't forget if you need somebody to carry your bags..."

Nancy nearly jumped down the phone at me.

"Oh, Mama, I was hoping you would say that. I really think I could make it if you were there as well. Two heads are better than one and I think it will give me the courage I need to start up if you're there too."

I was not expecting that response and had only made the remark in jest. However, Nancy was not going to let me off so lightly.

"But, I couldn't give my job up, Nancy, and what about the house? I could certainly come out for a holiday and help."

"Can't you take unpaid leave for six months? And you can rent your house out whilst you're away, you could still pay the mortgage."

"Well, I'm not sure if work will let me do that, darling. Yes, I could rent the house out, but I can't just give my job up, but I will ask if they do career breaks and let you know."

They did and so it was finalised at work that I would take six months unpaid leave from November until May. Renting the house was not so easy, nobody wanted to rent short term for those specific months and so I took a mortgage break and left the house empty whilst my other daughter, Josie, and the neighbours kept an eye on it. Now, this all seems quite simple when put down on paper, but in fact it was quite a challenge for me. I am not normally so adventurous. I have travelled widely, but only for two or three week holidays. I once lived in New York for six months, but this was many years ago when I was married and when my eldest daughter, Josie, was a baby, before Nancy was born. To leave my job and live in India for six months was daring by my standards, but lately I had been longing for something different and here it was offered to me on a plate, I had to accept.

4

Nestled Amongst Temples

I was 54 years old; I had been divorced for over 25 years and brought my two daughters up on my own since they were small. Josie was now 31 and Nancy 29. I worked as a university lecturer in the Faculty of Health and Social Care. I liked my job, but, due to the economic climate, there were additional pressures creeping in and at this time in my life I was tired and in need of refreshment for the soul. I had a year to prepare myself for India. Nancy visited Goa from Mumbai on several occasions during the year and put a deposit on a small house for us to rent in Arpora. She sent me photographs of the house; it had an extremely basic kitchen, ceilings with open rafters, and a charming little red veranda. I was smitten, and showed the photographs to friends, students, and work colleagues. I could not wait to leave. I envisaged myself doing daily yoga and meditation, perhaps undertaking a teacher's training course in yoga, this being something that I already practiced at home, but due to other commitments only on a weekly basis; however, this could all change. I imagined myself meeting spiritual people in Goa, having more time to socialise and make strong friendships, perhaps falling in love again. It was going to be a very spiritual time I felt. Oh, it was all possible, I just could not wait to go and the months slowly took their time to pass, but eventually, as always, they did.

During the year leading up to my departure, Nancy and I had many discussions in regard to the company, not least about the name we were going to give it. We debated several names and finally decided upon MamaNoo. Nancy and Josie had always called me Mama for some unfathomable reason and as a child Nancy had been nicknamed Noodlepippin which had got shortened to Noo along the years. So an amalgamation of the two names seemed to be as good as any for the company, not the most original of ideas perhaps, but workable we thought. It is strange how a name takes on a life of its own with time. Take a newborn baby for instance, who just does not suit the given name of Harry or Charles or Lisa or Heidi, but with the passage of time they start to own the name, so much so that eventually it appears to be the only name they do suit. So MamaNoo began to take root; at first the name seemed a little silly and frivolous and it was almost an embarrassment to say to people, but with time it took on a grandeur of its own and embarrassment was overtaken by pride when asked by somebody the company name. Likewise the company logo changed with time, at first Nancy had drawn a very arty Aztec design which spelled out MamaNoo on the company cards. However, as the business grew over the first six months, we changed the logo to a more sophisticated, italic styled writing with the name in gold on a black background. MamaNoo now represented a quality, designer product, whereas before it represented a fuzzy dream that was yet to materialise.

A couple of months before the leaving date, Nancy phoned me to say that she was delaying her date of leaving Mumbai for another three weeks, as there was a big exhibition that the company was preparing for and she had been asked to stay on to help. This meant that I would be in India for three weeks on my own. Now, I'm aware that this would not pose a problem for many people, but I am not one of them. I am not good at doing adventurous things alone. I have travelled abroad on my own to meet people on many occasions and this does not worry me, but to stay alone in a country that I am not familiar with filled me with anxiety. However, I was determined to go at the designated month and thought that I would fill my time by joining a yoga group, perhaps doing the teachers training course that I had envisaged. I was discussing the issue with my friend Kate, a previous work colleague, when she suggested that she accompany me for the first month and we could travel around India together until Nancy was able to join me in Goa. Problem solved, and so the tickets were booked.

Tourist visas for India only allowed for a six month stay at the maximum, so I booked my return ticket for exactly six months from the date I would be leaving the United Kingdom. However, I later discovered, when my visa arrived, that the stay is actually 180 days not six calendar months and so I had to purchase another return ticket home from Goa as I was four days over the allocated time. An expensive lesson to learn.

As Kate and I wanted to fly to India together, we discussed the option of buying a holiday for a month and I would forego the flight home. However, Kate discovered a site where scheduled flights were quite reasonable in price; and allowed for long intervals between return flights. What we failed to take into account, however, was that they were the flights from Hell. Three planes to travel from Manchester to Goa and long delays between connections, which meant that we would be travelling for almost 24 hours before reaching Goa. Nonetheless, ever the optimists we booked the flights, Kate to return in one month and myself in six months. Exciting. We decided to go straight to Goa, settle into the little house and then after about five days to go travelling for a few weeks then return to Goa at the same time as Nancy, towards the end of November. It was a loose kind of itinerary and one which we could alter to suit.

Chapter 2: The Little Red House

The weekend we arrived in Goa, Nancy had come down from Mumbai with an Indian friend Pataj, who had kindly driven her to the rented house in his car, loaded up with her belongings. She had arrived on the Friday and was returning on the Sunday. She met us at the airport in a taxi on the Saturday morning, dressed in jeans and a kurta and dupatta, the Indian dress and scarf ensemble. She wore the scarf Indian style, draped around her chest with the ends falling down her back. The outfit looked fabulous on her and with her dark hair and tanned skin she looked a beautiful fusion of east and west. She merrily informed us that she had been partying the previous night after cleaning and sorting out the house and had not yet been to bed. She looked remarkably well on it.

Unfortunately, I had mixed up the times of the flights and had texted Nancy from Amsterdam airport, where we had our first flight change, to inform her that we were arriving at 7:00 a.m. In fact we left Mumbai at that time and arrived at Dabolim Airport in Goa an hour later. The taxi driver appeared relaxed considering he had been waiting around the airport for 90 minutes, although Nancy quietly told me that she had assured him that we would pay extra for his inconvenience. Nancy introduced him to us as Santosh, and informed us that he was also

9

the landlord of our new home. Both Kate and I were shattered and longing for bed. Although it was morning, we decided in the taxi that we would go to bed for a few hours when we arrived at the house and then get up and go to sleep that evening at a normal hour. Hopefully, in this way we would acclimatise to the Indian time zone within the first day.

Nancy appeared anxious on the drive from the airport and was whispering to me on the back seat, so Santosh would not hear her and take offence.

"I hope you like the house, Mama, it's very basic, but it's got character, there's something about it."

"I'm sure that I'll love it, darling. It looks lovely on the photos, very authentic and rustic. I can't wait to see it."

"I spent all yesterday cleaning and tidying, but the floors still look grubby, it's the clay, it doesn't look clean."

"I'm sure it will be fine, don't worry, darling."

"I've made your beds up with clean sheets, and I've been shopping, so we can have a cup of tea and some biscuits when we arrive. I hope you like it."

We arrived in Arpora and Nancy announced, "We're here," as the car turned off a main road and onto a sloping dirt track by the side of a large temple which was presently only partly built and encased in bamboo scaffolding. The dirt track continued downhill, snaking between a cluster of more temples, both large and small and of various colours and designs. There were about a dozen in total and at the end of the incline, nestled cosily amongst the temples, was a little house with a sloping red roof and a pillar box red veranda with the Om symbol, painted in white, upon the gate posts. It was utterly,

utterly charming and soon earned the name of the House of MamaNoo or MamaNoo House.

We walked through the front gates of the veranda and Nancy opened the carved wooden front door. It opened into the front room where Nancy's friend Pataj was laying on a mattress on the floor, sleeping off the excesses of the previous night. We walked through the front room into a central room which contained a bed frame, and from this room two other rooms were accessed; a large back bedroom and a large dining room. To the rear of the dining room was a small kitchen and to the side of the kitchen was a toilet and shower room. The house had high ceilings and exposed roof beams with the underside of the roof tiles being visible. The floors were made of red clay and the walls of the house, both inside and out, were painted cream. The windows were barred with elaborate wrought iron patterns and had wooden shutters, but no glass. There was little furniture in the house; three iron bed frames with mattresses, a plastic table and two plastic chairs, a fridge, a portable two ring gas stove, and an old wooden table and bench. There were no cupboards or wardrobes but there was a large cubby-hole in the dining room which could be used for storage, although it lacked doors. In fact, apart from the front and back doors and the back bedroom, none of the rooms had doors just empty doorframes. Although not as appealing from the inside, the house, nonetheless, had a rustic charm to it. I liked it.

Kate and I had the promised cup of tea and biscuits and then went into the back bedroom where there were two beds, which Nancy had made up for us. There was no other furniture in the room, which had a low sloping ceiling with exposed beams and a small window with a wooden shutter. We were both exhausted after the long journey and thankfully got into the beds. It was like lying on a bed of lumpy concrete.

"What's your bed like, Kate?" I enquired covetously.

"Rock hard, what's yours like?"

The mattresses were about half an inch thick and were laid on rusty metal bed frames which dipped in the middle with age. Fortunately for us, we were so tired we slept anyway, although we both woke up with stiff backs and aching joints and the knowledge of what lay ahead for us night after night.

Nancy and Pataj left the next day to start the long drive back to Mumbai. Before leaving we made arrangements with Nancy to visit her in Mumbai in around a week's time when Kate and I would start our travels. Firstly, we wanted to enjoy a rest in Goa and recuperate from our journey before we started more travelling. Over the next few days, we set about on a mission to turn the little house into a home. This involved much scrubbing and cleaning, purchasing and arranging, and working wonders with a ball of string, a stack of bamboo canes, and lots of empty water bottles. Bamboo canes were tied together tepee style with a connecting length of cane across the top of two wigwams to become an open wardrobe. A bamboo ladder we found on the floor was placed against a wall in the back bedroom and became another avant garde wardrobe. The tops of water bottles were cut off and these became holders for pens, candles, cutlery, and kitchen utensils, whilst the larger bottles were chopped up and reclaimed as waste paper bins for the rooms. Kate came into her own in this department, covering some of the chopped bottles with cloth to pretty them up and burning holes in the sides, tying on string handles, and then placing them around the house and garden as tea light holders.

The bathroom was a particular horror for me as in the evening, once dusk had fallen, an army of ants would march from the toilet pipe, around the walls of the room and outside again. It was relentless. As a consequence, I hated going to the toilet or showering once it was dark, as thousands of ants joining me in that little room just gave me the creeps. So I commenced my war on ants, buying numerous insect sprays and squirting them incessantly, but still they marched on, a proud army defying defeat. Kate scrubbed the bathroom walls and toilet whilst I tackled the fridge, neither of the tasks enviable ones. She gaily informed me that when she sprayed around the shower head another army of ants emerged from that spot too and she suspected a nest in the walls of the room. Oh, joy!

Not having the luxury of waste collections in Goa, rubbish had to be burned which became my task. I made a bonfire in the back garden and all of the rubbish, apart from plastic bottles, tin cans, and glass was burnt there. It was strangely satisfying piling up the rubbish and then setting fire to it all, poking it with a stick to keep the air circulating. Whilst managing the bonfire, I also tidied the back garden by collecting more discarded litter that had accumulated there. By the end of the first week, the garden was looking rubbish free and consisted of nought but bare earth, the ashes of the bonfires, and a large pole which we presumed, by the smell, was for letting gasses out of the septic tank which held the toilet waste. Not knowing what to do with the empty bottles, cans, and jars we had used, I placed them in a box outside of the back door intending to ask the landlord when I next saw him. However, the box mysteriously disappeared overnight. We discovered that recycling is big in India where people are paid for providing the recyclable materials of glass, plastic, and metal. Sorted.

Whilst outside for my burning duties I found two large planks of wood which looked as though they had been part of an internal door at some point. I bought two cheap plastic stools and placed these against the back wall of the central room and laid the planks across them; this became our bookshelf and storage spot. In the front room, Nancy had left a huge bag of different materials which had been samples from the design company that she worked for. She had instructed us not to cut the materials as she intended using them, but told us that we could utilise them around the house. They were beautiful, some so expensive to produce that they never got beyond the sample stage. We had great fun hanging these luxurious materials at the windows and doorframes of our humble little home. It always made me smile when I entered the house to see the very basic front room with its noticeable lack of furniture boasting the most sumptuous, expensive embroidered linen curtain hanging in the doorframe. Likewise, the cheap plastic table in the dining room was covered with an exquisite, silk embroidered cloth that was strikingly gorgeous.

In our quest for home making, we took a rickshaw to Mapsa, the nearest large town about five miles away, to visit the busy market there. It was a hot day and the market was buzzing with people and activity. We wanted to buy some pillows and pillowcases as the ones at the house were ancient, lumpy, and unpleasant to lie on. We found a stall at the market that sold both items for a reasonable price after some initial haggling. The stallholder had a pillow on display for us to view, and we decided on six, two for each bed. He reached under his stall and brought out six pillows wrapped in plastic and tied these together for us to carry home. Happy with our purchase and tired of the market, the bustle, and the heat, we were finding our way out when we noticed a stall selling large baskets. We walked over and began admiring these, discussing how many we would need to store our various belongings. We settled a price for four baskets with the lady stallholder, however, at this point we noticed another style of basket to the side of the ones we were purchasing and decided we preferred these instead. Another lady came over and informed us of the price, which we agreed, unaware that these baskets belonged to a different stall. At this point in the proceedings a screaming row broke out between the two stallholders, with one pushing the other in the chest. Quickly we grabbed two of the original baskets shouting over the fracas that we would buy two from each stall or none at all. This agreement appeared to placate everyone and another stallholder, who had been watching the scene, began to laugh loudly, we turned around to look at her and found ourselves joining in the laughter, appreciating the humour of the incident. Soon the two stallholders were also roaring laughing with their arms around each other.

"Good friends, like you," one of them smilingly informed us, seemingly oblivious to the fact that she had just been screaming abuse in her dear friends face moments earlier.

The stallholders cheerily waved us off as Kate and I struggled under our loads. On arriving home, we put the baskets in pride of place and admired them, not so the pillows. On opening the plastic bags, the smell of damp and must was overpowering. The pillows had obviously been stored during the monsoon and become damp; they were far worse than the original pillows of the house and no matter how much I smeared them with patchouli oil, they still stank. We felt cheated.

As foreigners to India it appeared that we were fair game for swindling, and overpricing of products and services was a regular occurrence. At around seven o'clock every morning a loud horn would sound intermittently for around five minutes, so loud that it was impossible to sleep through. Kate, an early riser, went outside on the second day to investigate. There at the side of the road was a man standing next to his bicycle that held a large basket on the front; she discovered that he was selling freshly baked bread still warm from the oven. Delighted, she bought two rolls off him for 20 rupees and we had a lovely breakfast of fresh bread with butter and jam. The next day she went out for more of the same and joined a queue behind one of our neighbours whom she noticed received six rolls for the same amount of money. When it came to Kate's turn, she smilingly handed over her 20 rupees and said, "I'll have the same as she just had, please." From then on we were no longer treated as westerners, well, at least as far as the bread man was concerned.

Other peddlers came by the little red house on bicycles too selling their wares. We had the bucket man, the ice cream man, and the knife sharpener man. They would all loudly toot their horns to announce their arrival and people would open their doors or look over their garden walls to see which particular peddler had arrived.

We were very fond of the bucket man who would cycle along the dirt track, steering with one hand whilst squeezing his bike horn with the other, a huge array of every size, shape, and colour of plastic bucket and jug imaginable tied to his cycle. It was a miracle of human endurance how he managed to cycle with all these buckets and jugs constantly banging against his legs and the wheels of his bike. We were a regular customer of his as our washing was done by hand, simply leaving the clothes to soak in buckets of soapy water over night and rinsing out in the morning to peg on the washing line. No two hour cycle malarkey here! With three of us in the house, large plastic buckets were in demand. I particularly enjoyed pegging out dripping wet washing only to bring it in a couple of hours later, crisp and dry from the Indian sunshine and smelling divine. The only problem was that the sunshine bleached our clothes and after weeks of washing they all turned the same pale, murky, pink-grey hippie shade.

We were in the house one day when we heard a horn incessantly parping, so we went outside to see what was being sold. Walking along the road was a lady with a wicker basket on her head. We called her over and she came onto our veranda and took the basket down from her head, placing it on the bench of the veranda. Then, she carefully unwrapped a cloth from around a huge jar that contained honey including the honeycomb itself. In broken English, she explained that she had gathered the honey that morning from a nest inside a tree. She asked us to bring her something to put the honey into and we went into the house and returned with a clean jar. She then removed a pair of old fashioned weighing scales from her basket and placed the jar on these, she then carefully spooned honey into our jar, conscientiously pointing out to us that she would deduct the weight of the jar from the overall calculation. She slowly rewrapped her large jar of honey, put everything back into her basket, thanked us for our custom, and went on her way again, walking down the lane with the basket balanced on her head, parping her horn. We ate fresh bread and honey that lunchtime, a mere 200 rupees for the most delicious tasting sandwiches that I have ever sampled.

Chapter 3: The Ragamuffin Gang

Although nestled amongst temples, the little red house was part of a small neighbourhood, with other houses to both sides and the rear. We were the only westerners in the small community and obviously a source of great interest. Unlike the British, Indian people are not as reserved and our neighbours had no problem in stopping in front of the house to say "hello" when we were sat out on the veranda and then continuing to stand and stare at us unabashed, sometimes for as long as twenty minutes. The neighbourhood children also found us a source of great interest and would stand in front of the house and shout "hello" to us through the dining room window. We only had to say "hello" back and this was taken as an invitation for them to come onto the veranda. The child visitors fell into two distinct camps; teenage children of our Goan neighbours who owned the houses around us, and the younger children of migrant workers from the neighbouring state of Karnataka, who were here to work during the holiday season and rented rooms in the area. The older Goan children openly scorned and derided the younger children, who would cower and hide when they saw the teenagers. The older children were educated, spoke English, and wore fashionable western clothes, whereas the young Karnatikans went barefoot and wore dirty, tatty clothes. They wandered about the

19

little estate all day long, playing in and around the temples whilst their parents and older siblings worked. We nicknamed them the "Ragamuffin Gang." The eldest was a beautiful young girl aged ten called Laysa, who had the chore of caring for her younger brother Salim, of four years and baby sister Yasmi, who was around 12 months old and absolutely adorable. We would see Laysa wandering around the little estate with the baby on her hip, holding her brother's hand, with a small crowd of other children in tow; she was like the Pied Piper. In total there were around twelve children in the gang, the majority aged between three and six years, and they all visited our little house on a daily basis. They were unkempt, uneducated, poor, and very, very loveable.

We would play with them on the veranda, bringing out paper and coloured pens for them to write and draw with. They spoke little English so we conversed in simple words and sign language. We would sing songs for them with catchy tunes and they, likewise, for us. We taught them to count to ten in English and they taught us in Kannada, although they learnt their lessons well and we forgot ours quickly. We swapped names and ages and we showed them pictures of our homes and family. They loved having their photographs taken and would pose merrily for us and then scrabble to stare at the picture on the screen of the camera. They never appeared to have access during the day to either food or water and were always grateful for either, often asking for "pani, pani" the Hindi name for water and indicating with a thumb towards their mouths. They would quite often get overexcited when all of them were on the little veranda together and would start shouting and laughing loudly as children do. One of our neighbours, whose house faced the side veranda of ours, came across one day shouting at the children to go away and then turned to us yelling that he would not tolerate this noise any longer as his daughter was studying for her examinations and could not concentrate. His house was a distance away from the veranda and although the children were noisy, they were not as noisy as the neighbour's own dog who barked all night, along with the other dogs in the area. The tirade was shocking and seemed so hypocritical as he was a religious man and we would often see him early in the morning picking flowers off the bushes to take to the temples. These poor children had so very little and yet they were happy and joyful, but even this seemed to be resented by the neighbourhood home-owners. Nonetheless the children still visited, albeit with us hushing them, which would make them laugh and point to the neighbour's house. They were obviously used to the derision.

We answered a knock on the door soon after this episode, to be greeted by another neighbour who asked us if we would like to donate to the building of a new temple in the area, there were already 12 in the small vicinity. "How about collecting money for a school for the migrant workers' children?" I suggested. She feigned lack of comprehension; it was not her problem.

One day Laysa turned up at the house unaccompanied, it was the first time we had seen her without a baby on her hip and a horde of children around her. In limited English and with signs, we elicited that for some reason her sister of 14 had not gone to work that day and was looking after their siblings. We presumed that the rest of the gang were also with the sister. Delighted that Laysa had been unburdened from her duties we invited her into the house, something that we had not done before with the children. In her shy, respectful way we could tell that she was delighted. She sat with us at the dining room table and carefully drew and coloured pictures with total concentration. She lunched with us and, with no prompting, assisted with clearing the table. We would not let her help to wash up which she wanted to do. This was her day of rest and we wanted this beautiful little ten year old girl to have time she could cherish. We gave her string and beads and she sat making necklaces that we admired. She had a beam on her face and her eyes danced with pleasure. She stayed with us for around two hours and then announced that she would have to go home.

We were never quite sure if the children told their parents that they visited us, but we suspected not. We would see them sometimes with their parents visiting the temples, but they always looked down quickly and would not meet our eye in order to avoid greetings. We reasoned that they had been told never to interact with strangers, as they were left alone all day and anything could happen. They were incredibly vulnerable.

One of the neighbourhood teenagers, who befriended us, from our first day, was Rakmir, who was 17 years old and very handsome. His family were quite affluent and owned a taxi service and a garage in Anjuna the nearest town. Rakmir was training to be a mechanic. He gave us his mobile phone number and proudly asserted that if there was anything we needed he could sort this for us. He was as good as his word arranging Indian SIM cards for our mobile phones and a dongle to enable internet access. He would also tell us the prices we should be paying for items when we went shopping on the markets, so that we were not overcharged. He had been driving since he was 14 years old he told us and although he did not hold a license, he regularly drove us into town in the family's rickshaw taxi. His older brother drove the car taxi and as they lived locally it was almost like having a chauffeur on call whenever we needed to go anywhere. Rakmir would pop round on a daily basis to see if there was anything we needed and although his prices were not cheap, he was so accessible and handy that we used him constantly. Quite the young entrepreneur.

*

Almost from our arrival at the little house, we were visited by an assortment of stray dogs and cows. It seemed that in our small neighbourhood almost every household owned a dog that was kept outside day and night and allowed to wander freely. The dogs would quite often gang together in a pack and it could be quite daunting when turning off the main road onto the dirt track which led to our house, to be confronted by a pack of barking and growling dogs. However, the dogs soon got to know us and became friendly, visiting us whenever we were sitting outside on the veranda of the house. Two regular canine visitors were Mangy Dog and Amber. Mangy Dog, so called by us because her fur was missing in places due to her constant scratching, belonged to a neighbour who lived at the back of us and also drove a rickshaw taxi. We soon discovered whose dog it was, as whenever the rickshaw drove past our house, Mangy Dog would give a bark of pleasure and jump over the veranda wall to chase the taxi home to greet her master. She was a very affectionate dog who was obviously well fed as she always refused any titbits we offered her, merely rolling over onto her back for more belly tickling which she loved. She had gentle eyes and was a sweet natured animal. All of the dogs had fleas and would scratch, but with Mangy Dog, this was incessant. Feeling quite sorry for Mangy Dog and her constant irritation, I bought some antiseptic spray for dogs from a local supermarket and treated her with it, reasoning that her owner would never know. Unfortunately, the spray was turmeric based, a popular treatment in India for skin conditions, and resulted in turning Mangy Dog's bald areas a bright yellow, which would not come off even with soap and water. No hiding that one! However, if her owner was disturbed that we were interfering with his dog he never showed it, still waving gaily whenever he saw us.

Another visitor of the canine variety was Amber, who was only a young dog of around a year old. She was a beautiful caramel colour with the most gorgeous golden eyes, hence the name we gave her. The street dogs of India tend to be of medium height and slim build with large pointed ears and a variety of colours. Amber was of a larger build than most, but quite slim. The children told us that she was a stray dog, but that she often slept outside of one of the neighbour's houses as the family sometimes gave her scraps to eat. She was always ravenous and we took to buying her tinned pilchards as these were cheap and nutritious and she loved them, continuing to lick the bowl for a good ten minutes after she had scoffed down the contents in around ten seconds.

I had been determined when first realising that there were so many stray animals around and about, that I would not get emotionally attached to any of them. Yes, I would pat them, yes, I would even feed them, but no, I would not fall in love with any of them. I think though, of all the animals, Amber was the one whom I had the most problems with not getting too attached to. She began to regard us as her family, barking in joy whenever she saw us and bounding after us. She was large and clumsy and would often leap right over the veranda wall, so overjoyed to see us as we stepped out of the house, only to send a glass of juice or a cup of tea through the air to soak the nearest recipient. She would also jump up at us constantly and no matter how often we taught her to "sit" and "get down" she would still jump whenever she got excited, almost knocking us over on occasions. She began to sleep on the veranda during the day and would bark or scratch at the door to be let in. If we ignored her, she would eventually stop it and settle down to sleep for a while or wander off.

The dogs having slept through most of the day due to the heat, became quite active at night and would gather together in packs and roam around the little neighbourhood. Every night they would bark and howl and it took a long time before I was able to acclimatise to this noise at night and eventually switch off to it and fall asleep. Amber was the worst of the barking culprits and we would hear her in the early hours of the morning, barking longer and louder than all of her companions. Sometimes she would take to howling; a sad haunting noise which seemed to contain all the misery of the world in one piercing sound. The other dogs would join in until eventually an angry neighbour whose house they were sat outside would yell or throw a bucket of water over the dogs and they would disperse into the dark to start barking again in a few minutes. It was a nightly chorus.

The large temple at the top of the dirt track was still being built when we moved into the house and was at the stage of having a plaster coating rendered over the bricks. A group of artisans from across India were brought in to work on decorating the plaster. They were housed in a small building opposite the temple and must also have taken to feeding Amber, because she began to alternate between sleeping on our veranda and sleeping in a large pile of sand which was outside the artisans' house. She could see our front garden from this spot and would spy us in the morning as we came outside onto the veranda to eat breakfast. Delighted she would bound up and dive over the veranda wall and onto our knees, knocking breakfast plates out of our hands. Protesting angrily we would push her onto the floor where she would merrily shake herself down, scattering sand all over the food and us. It became a regular occurrence, neither parties ever learning their lessons.

Amber did not like sharing our affections with any of the other neighbourhood dogs and set about fighting with Mangy Dog one day, when she had jumped over the veranda wall and found her there. Mangy Dog ran off quickly and Amber chased her growling, we hastily followed and pulled the dogs apart, but Mangy Dog was bleeding and limped off home with her tail between her legs, literally. Mangy Dog never visited us again after this, although if we saw her on the road she always came up to us, wagging her tail and rolling over, eager for a little belly rub.

*

In India the cows are sacred animals and allowed to roam freely. Hordes of them casually wander along the streets oblivious to the traffic, sauntering lazily across roads whilst cars and bikes come to a screeching halt. Quite often people put vegetable scraps outside of their houses for the cows to eat and they are seen amongst the houses and gardens looking for titbits. The first week we were in the house, Kate and I were sitting on the veranda one evening when a cow wandered into the garden and poked its head over the veranda gate. It had one horn almost horizontal to its head and one almost vertical, like a letter L. We christened it Lopsy.

Lopsy was heavily pregnant and huge, her enormous belly swaying from side to side as she slowly walked along with the bones of her back jutting out in sharp contrast. Although quite urban, the cows are not normally friendly and avoid contact with people, but Lopsy was obviously hungry. I went into the house and came out with a watermelon and a bunch of coriander, which were the only suitable foods in the fridge. She wolfed them both down in a few seconds, slurping the watermelon with obvious enjoyment. After that evening, she visited us every evening that week for supper, but then Kate and I went travelling and the house was left empty.

We did not get any more visits from Lopsy on our return to the house after our travels and we wondered what had happened to her, worrying that she might have died whilst birthing. However, a few weeks after we had come back to the house, we were returning home one day and spotted Lopsy at the top of the dirt track just off the main road. It was definitely Lopsy, there was no mistaking those horns, but she was thin and no longer pregnant. We looked around to see where her calf was, but she was on her own. She started to visit us now and again and would sometimes just poke her head over the veranda wall for a head scratch, which she loved, grunting with pleasure as we scratched between her eyes and down her face. We never found out what happened to her calf, but we reasoned that it must have been stillborn. When we finally came to leave, six months later, Lopsy was obviously pregnant again. The circle of life playing itself out.

Chapter 4: Manic Mumbai

Kate and I stayed for almost a week at MamaNoo House and transformed it in that time, so that it looked quite homely when we left to go travelling, making us feel reluctant to go. We flew to Mumbai and made arrangements to be picked up by Nancy at the airport. Mumbai was a complete and utter culture shock to me, for although I had travelled widely, I had never in my life experienced anything quite like this. Nancy had a car provided by her company and so she drove to the airport to collect us. The traffic was horrendous and how she could drive in it after only knowing the relative calm and organisation of British roads left me in admiration. Although the main roads had designated lanes, nobody appeared to take any notice of these, and at one point on the drive back to Nancy's apartment, I counted eight cars spread widthways across four lanes. Cars drove bumper to bumper with rickshaws weaving in and out hazardously. Everybody appeared to be honking their horns and the noise was intolerable. As Nancy noted at one point, when Kate and I were in amazed panic at the driving, "Don't worry, if we crash it won't be serious because you can't get any speed up in this traffic." The air was foggy with fumes and although it was hot in Mumbai I noticed that most cars had their windows shut.

29

Alongside the fumes of Mumbai was the smell of decay which was evident in parts throughout the city due, I concluded, to the litter that was visible everywhere, with piles of it accumulating at roadsides and against buildings in some places. There did not appear to be any litter-bins or collections provided by the city and so rubbish was burnt or simply discarded in the streets. The rains of the monsoon and the fumes of the traffic gave the buildings a mouldy black coating that added to the initial shock when viewing the city. Although these sites were surprising, they were nothing in comparison to witnessing the poverty of Mumbai. Whole families were sleeping on pavements at the side of roads and under overpasses. On one main road I witnessed a family camped out with a little toddler wandering in the gutter and the crazy drivers of Mumbai whizzing past. I had heard about the Dharavi slums in Mumbai before I arrived, but it seemed to me now that the slum dwellers were one step further up the ladder than these poor souls. I could not understand why they should choose to camp out at that particular spot; why not choose a quieter road where traffic and fumes were more bearable? I could only conclude that this was due to reasons of safety, they were in full view of hundreds of people.

However, alongside the dirt, traffic and biting poverty was evidence of sheer opulence and wealth. There were plenty of elegant grand hotels and modern chic restaurants; the main roads were lined with designer shops and boutiques with elaborate window displays, and the traffic was interspersed with numerous expensive, chauffeur driven limousines. It was definitely a city of contrasts and opposites.

Nancy's apartment was in Bandra, a suburban upmarket neighbourhood that mainly consisted of apartment blocks, shops, and restaurants. Her apartment was beautiful with marble flooring and an enormous sitting room with a balcony that overlooked the street below. It had four bedrooms, each with an en-suite, and she shared it with three other flatmates, all British designers working for the same company. The girls were welcoming to us and we felt at home. Nancy gave us her bedroom, which contained a large king sized bed, whilst she slept on one of the sofas in the sitting room. She was thrilled that I was there and informed me that I was the only parent of the European designers that had visited. The girls assured us that the initial shock of the city would dissipate with time and that we would soon become acclimatised to it. Nancy, in an effort to show us the nicer side of the city, booked high tea at the Taj Mahal Hotel in Colaba, which was south of the city. We took a rickshaw from her apartment which was in the west of the city and were afforded a clear demonstration of how large Mumbai was, as it took almost an hour in moving traffic to reach our destination.

*

We stayed in Mumbai for a week and then left to fly to Jaipur in Rajasthan. We enquired about catching a train, as I was anxious about money knowing that I had only a limited amount of savings to last the six months. Besides, I reasoned, train travel would allow us to see more of the country. However, all of the trains were fully booked as it was the festival of Diwali and many Indians were travelling to see friends and family. Kate preferred to fly and did not want to travel by coach when I suggested this, and so we left Mumbai by air. We stayed in a hotel that Nancy had booked for us at work, as we were unable to get onto the internet in her apartment due to problems with the connection. The hotel, although not cheap, was basic and tired looking, but we decided to stay anyway as it was adequate and we did not want the hassle of looking elsewhere. The elderly bellboy showed us to our room; he was small, thin, and dressed in a khaki uniform which was far too large for him. He had a military posture and was extremely formal, demonstrating the light switches, the shower, the door lock, and the television in our room with a certain pomp, as if it were a grand hotel. Kate and I struggled not to giggle.

After a little relaxation in our room we went into the lounge which was on the ground floor. It was a dark, cheerless place in the middle of the building with no windows and hard wooden furniture. A sign on the wall announced that beer was served here. The same bellboy arrived to take our order, we asked for two beers. He looked flabbergasted and asked us to repeat the order. Again, we asked for two beers.

"Beer? Beer?" he asked confused.

We assured him that yes, that was what we wanted and we pointed towards the sign on the wall. Still confused he walked over to the sign and touched the word beer. We both nodded enthusiastically. He looked dismayed and came back to the table whispering, "Beer? Beer very strong!"

"Good," I said. "I like strong beer."

He looked even more taken aback and went off to get our order. When he returned with the two bottles, he uncapped them with great ceremony and slowly poured them for us. He placed Kate's glass in front of her and then mine, and leaning over to me he gave me one last warning: "Beer very strong." Kate and I could no longer contain our giggles; they erupted like an overflowing volcano.

In Jaipur we did the tourist trail and visited palaces, forts, temples, and an amazing outdoor observatory with huge observational instruments. We had intended catching a train to Agra to visit the Taj Mahal, but, of course, the trains were fully booked here too. After much deliberation, we decided to get a taxi to the Taj the next day, stay overnight in a hotel, and then get the taxi back the following day; as it was an all day drive. The receptionist at the hotel in Jaipur was very helpful and informed us that this was feasible, but also informed us that we would not be reimbursed for the night we had booked at our present hotel. It was an expensive trip and Kate seemed reluctant to spend two days in a taxi, but this was one of the wonders of the world and we were so near. I persuaded her to go with me and it was so worth it.

The Taj Mahal was breathtakingly beautiful. As we walked through the entrance gates, the sight of the building made me gasp. Our guide informed us that the marble changes colour with the time of day and the seasons. We had arrived around four o'clock in the afternoon and the sun was low in the sky turning the marble to a beautiful pale, creamy pink colour, it was simply and utterly awe inspiring. I kept touching the walls of the mausoleum hoping that some of the love that inspired the building would rub off on me. There were crowds of people visiting and although we queued to take a picture of each other sat on the famous seat where Diana Spencer, Princess of Wales had wowed the world, there were just too many people jostling for the same position. Instead we struck Diana poses standing in front of the building, head lowered and eyes looking up at the camera. Kate won hands down at the pose, she had the shy, winsome look off pat and I just had to admit defeat with this one.

Differences in culture between east and west became apparent, once again, at the entrance to the Taj Mahal. The payment booths at the gates were divided into two; one for Indian nationals with an entrance fee of 20 rupees and one for foreigners with an entrance fee of 750 rupees. I could not imagine politically correct Britain arriving at a similar scheme.

After a stay of around a week, we flew back to Mumbai to visit Nancy once again. She had procured an interview for a freelance design post with an Italian company based in India who specialised in embroidery. They had several famous companies as clients and although Nancy was excited, she was unsure if she really wanted the extra burden of freelance work when she was starting her own company. The interview was in Bangalore and Kate and I decided to fly there with her to visit the state of Karnataka. Nancy was finishing her job in Mumbai that week and needed to pack her belongings that she had not already taken to Goa. She assured us that there was not a lot to pack, but having stayed in her bedroom we were not convinced of this as it was overflowing with clothes, shoes, books, jewellery, and a beautiful carved hardwood chair.

Nancy had found the chair in the storeroom of the apartment, where it had been abandoned because the seat was broken. It belonged to the dining room set, but this already had eight chairs, so it was an additional one. Nancy reasoned that her landlord would neither repair nor miss the chair, so she had it renovated with the seat covered in a beautiful mustard linen material which was embroidered with huge pink chrysanthemums, another sampler from the company that she worked for. The chair was stunning. She intended taking it to Goa to have it as a showpiece on the market stalls. Her friend Pataj would not let her take it with them when they visited, as he did not want to damage his car with it; so she was going to post it from Mumbai to our landlord's house in Goa where she could collect it. She informed us that the post office had a wrapping service.

We all set off one day, chair in tow, to find a large taxi to take us to get the chair wrapped and posted. The chair was heavy and burdensome, so we all took turns to carry it. The easiest way to hold it and walk was with the back of the chair facing you, but the legs of the chair banged against your own legs making it a painful procession. The crowded streets of Mumbai did not allow for two of us to carry it together. There was no way we were all going to fit into a rickshaw and large taxi cars were few and far between. We eventually found one big enough to fit all of us and our treasure; but we arrived at the post office to be told that the chair was too large to post. We would have to send it by courier. Apparently, there was a courier service nearby, so we set off again with the chair in tow; by now all of our legs were showing scars from the ordeal and we were roasting hot, carrying our load in the midday sun. We arrived at the couriers to be informed again that they would not touch it as it could not be insured and, besides, they only sent parcels.

We set off again for another courier, who told a similar tale. By this time, we were all fed up, tired, and hot. We sat down inside the courier's office on the chair and Nancy whispered,

"You get this in India, if it's too much trouble they just won't help. It's not their company, so they don't care about the business. Let's insist."

So insist we did. We just kept repeating that this was a courier service and we wanted an item couriering. Running out of excuses the man behind the counter eventually said;

"But it's not wrapped." It was a chink in his armour and we dived in.

"Then we'll wrap it," we informed him.

We insisted that the chair was left there and we went off to buy bubblewrap, cardboard, scissors, and sellotape. We came back and, in the midday sun, set about wrapping the chair outside of the shop. Next door was a petrol station and people were staring at us as we set about our task. Surprisingly, it took the three of us around half an hour, as every leg and the two arms were individually bandaged first with bubblewrap and then with cardboard; we did an excellent job. At one point, the man behind the desk came out to join us; all three of us laughing so much that it must have looked great fun.

Feeling quite elated that we had finally sent the chair off we decided to go for something to eat and drink. We were in a main thoroughfare and there were plenty of restaurants within walking distance. Kate and Nancy were talking together as we walked and I was slightly ahead of them. As I stopped at the kerb of a main road to cross over, a cyclist veered towards me with a strange leer on his face. As I looked I realised that his trousers were tucked under his penis and testicles, and these were on show; he was fully erect. He leered at me and then pedalled on.

"Oh my God, did you see that, did you see that?" I shrieked at Kate and Nancy who were coming up behind me.

"See what?" they asked.

"That guy on the bike, he had his dick and everything hanging out. Well it wasn't hanging actually!"

They had not seen and for the rest of the day and indeed that week, I was teased mercilessly. The taunting took the flavour that like a thirsty man in a desert sees a mirage of water, I was seeing a mirage of erect penises. Ha ha, very funny!

I did not see any more mirages in India, despite our visit to a haberdashery bazaar the next day, which was the most crowded area imaginable. Nancy had decided that we needed more goods to sell on the market stalls in Goa and had rationalised that we could make our own jewellery cheaply. We had little initial funds so this was one way of bulking out our stock for only a small investment. We caught a rickshaw to the area which consisted of a maze of back streets and little shops, all selling hundreds upon hundreds of beads in every size, shape, and colour imaginable. It was an Aladdin's cave of treasures. There were throngs of people lining the streets; porters carrying bales of materials, ox carts pulling heavy loads, and cars jostling for space amongst street sellers who had set up their stalls in any space available. We went from shop to shop buying beads and accessories to make pendants, hair slides, earrings, and handbag charms. In total we spent around 40 pounds sterling; we could have multiplied that by 100 if we had bought them in Britain.

We arrived back at Nancy's apartment tired but happy with our day at the bazaar; it was our last night before the flight to Bangalore in the morning and Nancy had yet to pack. It soon became apparent that there was no way her luggage was going to fit into one suitcase, so Kate and I went out to buy two extra bags which were expandable and huge. We helped her to pack and we managed to fit everything into the two bags and her suitcase, but only after she had discarded a lot of her belongings. Luckily, Kate and I were travelling with hand luggage only, so we could take her cases as our hold luggage.

"You couldn't have got all of this on the plane if Kate and I weren't coming with you." I pointed out to Nancy. "What would you have done then?"

"Well you're here, so I'm sorted." She answered cockily.

Nevertheless, we were all on tenterhooks, wondering if the luggage would be over the allocated flight allowance. We checked in and it was just under; luck was on Nancy's side again.

Chapter 5: Back by Bus

We stayed in a modern hotel in the outskirts of Bangalore, the three of us sharing one room with twin beds and a camp style bed next to these that the porter erected for us. With the extra bed and the luggage we were very cramped. Nancy started to sort out her outfit for the interview and had decided upon wearing some silver earrings that I had bought for her in Mumbai as a thank you present for her hospitality. She pressed and hung up her clothes so that they were ready for the morning, but could not find one of the earrings. She emptied the contents of the bags all over the room, at which point I noticed that Kate had sensibly switched off to this panic and lay quietly reading her book. Nancy was frantic in her quest to find the earring. I joined in and also unpacked all of the bags that she had just finished ramming everything back into. Two hours later we had to admit that the earring must have been left in Mumbai.

First thing in the morning Nancy disappeared to attend the interview whilst Kate and I explored Bangalore. We met at the hotel in the evening to travel back to Goa together. As Nancy and I were keen to conserve money and the trains were fully booked, we had decided to book the overnight coach to Goa to travel back. It would take 16 hours. Although Kate did not say too much about this arrangement, I could tell that she was not thrilled with the plans, but I reasoned that she could fly back on her own if it was really a problem for her. Nancy and I had no salary for the next six months; we had to be sensible with our savings and besides this felt like a bit of an adventure. The hotel receptionists had assisted me with booking the coach online. The photographs on the website looked good, nice clean coaches with roomy bunks to sleep on. We would be fine.

We arrived at the coach station loaded up with Nancy's luggage once again and awaited our coach's arrival. Arrive it did and it was a rickety old boneshaker of a vehicle which bore no resemblance whatsoever to the photographs on the website. I put on a brave face but did not dare look at Kate. We stored our luggage in the hold and clambered on board. There were bunks, two beds high, lining the coach, double on one side and single on the other. Kate and I shared a lower double and Nancy was opposite the aisle in a lower single. The beds had sheets on them and a small pillow, with a folded blanket. I covered my sheet and pillow with a scarf; it didn't look as though it had been changed since the last passenger had slept on it; well, maybe the last ten actually. The journey was tough and sleep was impossible. Not only was the bus old and rickety, but the roads were potholed and uneven. To say it was a bumpy ride would be a huge understatement. The bus driver had a secret desire to be a rally contestant and kept his foot flat down on the accelerator the whole journey, with the consequence that when potholes were encountered we were bounced clean off the bunks and into the air. The descent onto a one inch thick mattress was not a pleasant experience. When encountering bends, he would swing the bus around with gusto, so much that it almost drove on two wheels, we had to ride holding onto the sides of the bunks to prevent being flung onto the floor. To add to the misery of the journey there were designated toilet breaks along the way, approximately every four hours, which meant that if you wanted to go in between these times there was no option but to wait with the added torture of being bounced about. It was a long 16 hours.

We sat up for most of the journey. I did not want to lie down because I had spotted several cockroaches and the thought of these creatures crawling over me whilst I slept was abhorrent. I did not mention this to my travel companions as I did not want to add more misery to their journey, but as it turned out, they had spotted them anyway and also kept mum. Nancy did sleep some of the journey, but Kate and I were awake throughout. To pass the time we devised a game in which we had to suggest alternative uses for a dupatta, the long scarf which is worn by Indian women and which I was presently using as a sheet. We had bought several in Mumbai and were quite taken with them. We took it in turns to suggest uses and the winner was the person with the last suggestion. The game took several hours on and off, with some ingenious suggestions, such as a sieve, sling, towel, and bag and just when we thought we had a winner, the opponent would eventually come up with a new suggestion and the competition was on again. We roared laughing along the way as we tried to suggest impossible uses for the scarf when it came to our turn and continually challenged each other's suggestions. Fatigue added to the hysteria.

At about four o'clock in the morning, the coach stopped on a main road for a toilet break. Both Kate and I had been awaiting this break for at least two hours as the bus was roasting hot, not having the promised luxury or air conditioning, and we had been drinking water to quench our thirsts. We gratefully rushed off the bus to discover that we were at the side of a main road with no buildings in the vicinity. Kate looked around us and then boarded the bus to ask the driver where the toilet was. He smiled patiently and opening both his palms upwards and shrugging, he looked about him as if to say "wherever you like." With the street lights shining on us we were in full view of the whole bus, either from the side windows or the front and back windows. We were both bursting to pee.

"I could hold my scarf up to cover you whilst you go." I offered. We both looked at each other and yelled "screen" simultaneously and broke into peals of laughter. It was yet another use for our multi-purpose dupatta.

We stopped a few hours later at a garage to fill the coach with fuel. Kate and I once again disembarked to find a toilet, whilst Nancy, with the bladder of youth, slept on. The attendant informed us that there was a toilet to the rear of the garage. It was still night and pitch black once we ventured around the back; by the light of a mobile phone and following the smell of excrement and stale urine we found a door that we pushed open, the stench was overpowering. There were no light switches to be found and the dim mobile phone light pointed towards the dark recesses of the room illuminated a squat pot; the hole in the floor style toilet that is common in India. I had been suffering from diarrhoea on and off for days now and, unfortunately, my stomach had been griping throughout the journey. There was no way that I was going to squat in that dingy, stinking, hell hole with

God only knows what insects and creatures lurking in its depth.

"I'm going out here," Kate announced after viewing the throne.

It was a sensible solution, but not when you are suffering with diarrhoea. Next to the squat pot was a plastic bucket which contained water and is used in India for washing, in place of toilet paper. I dragged it nearer to the door.

"I'm going in this" I said and left the door ajar slightly to ease the fear of claustrophobia and to allow for some fresh air to enter.

We got back onto the bus and settled into our bunk.

"Oh God, I've just had a thought," Kate said.

"What?"

"Can you imagine the next person to use that loo in the dark?"

"What do you mean?"

"They're going to wash themselves with the contents of that bucket!"

"Oh God, I should have emptied it...I just never thought. I just couldn't wait to get out of there."

We looked at each other in horror and then the laughter arrived. We laughed so much that we snorted for breath, which set us off again. We were hysterical, holding our sides due to the pain of laughing. We were tired, sore from being bounced around, definitely out of our comfort zones; it seemed to be a recipe for total and utter meltdown.

*

We eventually arrived in Panjim, Goa, at around midday, and we were shattered. We wearily found a taxi large enough to take us and all of Nancy's luggage back to our little house. Halfway through the taxi journey, Nancy announced that she had left her mobile phone on the bus.

"Call the phone, Mum, and we'll see if anyone answers."

The phone rang out, nobody answered. We asked the driver to turn the taxi around and go back to the coach station. I tried the number again, this time the call went straight to voice mail; the SIM card had been removed. We arrived back at the coach station and spoke to the staff, but they denied seeing the phone. The cleaner was on the coach when we arrived, but he simply claimed not to have seen it. There was nothing we could do, it was tempting to ask him to empty his pockets, but we did not. We gave my phone number in case it turned up and left feeling disappointed. It was a new Blackberry, her third that year; Nancy was good at mislaying phones. We had only been in the house around an hour when my phone rang. It was the coach station and Nancy's phone had been found. She got a taxi back to pick it up, apparently it had been found on the coach; the SIM card was back in place. We suspected that the cleaner had been searched, not too roughly we hoped.

It was lovely to be back at our little house and we decided to move my bed into the middle room so that we all had our own space. Nancy would sleep in the front room and Kate, on her own now, in the large back bedroom. It meant that both Nancy's room and mine would become walkways for access to other rooms, but this was not really a problem for us. I had bought two mosquito nets with me from England thinking that Nancy would have her own. She did not like them as it happened as they gave her a feeling of being closed in. Kate and I draped ours from the beams and they gave our ferociously hard beds a regal, princess look that belied their unrelenting cruelty.

One morning Kate appeared subdued and not her usual lively self.

"Are you all right?" I asked.

"Not really, no."

"What's up, honey?"

"I don't know if I should tell you this, but I'm pretty sure I saw a rat in the rafters of my room last night. I've been awake all night, I just couldn't sleep."

"Are you sure it was a rat, Kate? There are loads of chipmunks around, I saw some on the roof of the house next door yesterday."

We managed to convince ourselves that it was definitely a chipmunk that Kate had seen. Now why it should be easier to bear the idea that we had chipmunks in our rafters rather than rats, I do not really know as both are rodents. Somehow though, we viewed chipmunks as little and cute, whereas rats were just repulsive and vile.

It was about this time that we started noticing other creatures in and around the house. I was taking a towel out of a basket one day when there underneath were two of the most enormous cockroaches I have ever seen. They were like small tortoises they were so huge. Far too large to squash, we had to brave ourselves and empty the basket outside amidst much shrieking, shuddering, and running on the spot.

The Portuguese had invaded Goa in previous centuries and the house was built in the popular

Portuguese style with tall, thick walls on which the beams of the roof were laid and on top of these were placed the roof tiles. Not only was this very picturesque, with the ceilings of the house being very high and having wooden beams and clay tiles, but it also had the added benefit of keeping the house lovely and cool throughout the day. Hot air would rise and escape through the gap at the top of the walls where the rafters were laid. This gap was around six inches to a foot depending on the thickness of the beams. However, there were drawbacks as we were beginning to discover. The gap was an open invitation to insects and the smaller furry creatures in the vicinity. One time we left the breadbasket on the kitchen table overnight only to discover in the morning that its contents had been half eaten by something. Scary!

It seemed that our visitors did not plague everybody though. Kate was a smoker and would take a chair from the dining room onto the little back porch accessed from this room, to sit, read, and smoke her cigarettes. The porch was next to a dirt track and she was afforded a clear view of the comings and goings of the migrant workers who passed by on a shortcut across the fields and into the town. They were mainly women and would be dressed in bright saris carrying large baskets balanced perfectly on their heads. They were friendly and chatty although few spoke any English and we never knew what they were saying to us. Through sitting on the porch, Kate also became quite friendly with Pashkar, the lady of the house opposite. During the festival of Diwali, she arrived at our front door with a large plate of little fancies and nibbles that she had made and kindly insisted on leaving these with us to eat. They were delicious and must have taken hours of preparation. At this time we were being bitten mercilessly by mosquitoes in the house in the evenings and although we tried everything to prevent this, plug-ins, sprays, and lotions, still they attacked us. Our arms and legs were covered in swollen spots from their bites. Not a good look! Kate was chatting to Pashkar one day and mentioned the problems with mosquitoes and asked her advice on how to deter them.

"I don't know" she said dismissively, "I don't have mosquitoes in my house."

The inference was clear, mosquitoes do not venture into the houses of the elite. That clearly put us in our place. I challenged Kate to ask her how to eradicate rats, but she did not pick up my gauntlet.

*

Not all of our little visitors to the house were unwelcome, however. We had a gecko in every room of the house and these were marvellous little creatures for devouring the ubiquitous mosquitoes that arrived as soon as the sun set. The geckos were extremely respectful, quickly paddling to the top of the walls when we entered the rooms. We had names for them; Fred, a larger pale gecko lived on the back wall of the dining room and little Voyeur was our resident bathroom gecko. It was surprising that he was so small considering he had an army of ants to feast upon. When entering the bathroom he would peep at us shyly from the farthest corner of the room. There was a definite curiosity to his gaze, however this could have been more to do with our bathroom antics than with our bodies.

Water for the house was drawn from a spring well located to the side of the front veranda. There was a nod to modernity with an electric pump, however not so cutting edge that we had a system installed for heating the water. The water tank was on the roof of the house, which meant that by the afternoon the sun's rays had warmed its contents and showering at this time was a pleasant experience. However, showers were usually needed first thing in the morning when the water temperature was slightly above freezing. Now there were various methods of getting through this ordeal, none of which required lingering any longer than was absolutely necessary. I favoured the sing-made-up-songs-very-loudly technique, whilst I noticed that Nancy and Kate favoured a more shrieking come screaming approach. I kept meaning to give it a try to see if it improved the experience any. I never did acclimatise to cold showers.

Other cultural issues also became apparent as my stay in Goa progressed. The front garden of our little house was surrounded by a six-foot hedge. This had a gap of about four feet at the left-hand corner that was the entrance to the garden and the house. I had started to train the hedge at the top of this gap by tying the higher branches of the two hedges together, making a rather romantic entrance to the garden, especially as I started topiary, regularly trimming it into a heart shaped entrance. It was during one of my topiary sessions that I decided to trim the rest of the hedge too, where the branches were getting a little tall. In India, all of the Hindu houses have a temple in their garden built in honour of one of the gods and our house was no exception. In front of the hedge and opposite the front door of the house was a brightly painted square temple about two foot across and four foot high. It was in the usual style, being covered with sculptures of the deity of choice and built to hold a plant in the top. Getting carried away with my sharp knife and scissors, I decided that the tall, spindly plant it contained also needed a trim. I cut it down to about one inch high, reasoning that this would assist it to grow back thicker and be more aesthetically pleasing and in line with the hedge.

Soon after my enthusiastic pruning session, the landlord of the house came by on a courtesy visit. After checking that everything was fine with his tenants he left to go when he suddenly noticed the pruned temple bush.

"Whatever has happened?" he asked, examining the bush in horror.

"Ah, I pruned it so that it would grow back thicker," I said. "It wasn't looking very healthy."

"No," he said aghast. "You must never touch this, it is very bad luck for the house. Where is the plant?"

I showed him the remnants of the plant that I had cut; it was now black and dead. He looked further dismayed.

"Very bad luck," he muttered, "very bad luck. It is like your Jesus Christ and the cross —this is our religion, you should never touch this plant, never."

I felt dreadful and after he had gone, I soaked the amputated branches of the plant in water to assist them to root and then planted them back into the temple pot, hoping that they would grow. I watered them twice daily, but they did not revive, instead they stood in the pot, leafless and black, reminding me of my misdeed every time I noticed them when leaving the house.

We were to upset our landlord once again soon after this first occasion. One morning Kate and I were sat on the veranda when Nancy came outside with a picture frame in her hand.

"I forgot to show you this," she said, "I took it off the wall of the dining room when I cleaned the house before you arrived."

She passed us the frame and inside was a sepia print picture of a stern looking Indian women with grey hair scraped back, dressed in a sari and sat bolt upright on a dining chair. It had been taken in the front room of the house as we recognised the pattern on the clay floor in the picture.

"Who's this?" I asked. "I wouldn't like to mess with her." She looked foreboding, staring menacingly into the camera.

"I'm not sure, but I reckon it's Santosh's grandma; he said it was his grandmother's house."

We forgot all about the photograph and left it on the veranda when we went inside. Later that day, our landlord arrived and was shocked at seeing the photograph outside and, whether through fear or respect, insisted that it be hung back in the house. He explained that this was a picture of his grandmother, Matilda Chowdry, who originally owned the house; in truth it was an Indian name that sounded like Matilda to our western ears. As a compromise to his tenants, he hung the picture out of the way on a nail in the dining room cubby-hole in which we kept the sweeping brushes. From then on this became known affectionately as Matilda's Hole. Consequently, the following types of conversations would take place:

"Mum, have you seen my hula hoops?"

"Yes, I stuffed them into Matilda's Hole." It always made us chuckle.

Matilda was a woman of some standing in the community as, at a later date, Santosh mentioned that the land on which the temples were built had originally belonged to the house and Matilda had donated it all to the local community. Her initials, MC, were crafted into the wrought iron gates of the front and back veranda, and, by coincidence, these were also the initials of mine, Nancy's, and Kate's surnames as they all begin with the prefix Mc.

After this visit from the landlord, I kept finding myself thinking about Matilda in her cubby hole and felt impelled to move her to a more respectful position. So she was placed on the dining room wall, at the heart of the house. However, I still found that I was thinking about her, in fact it became more than thought, it was as though I could feel her presence on occasions. One day when I had gone native, sweeping the floors dressed in a sarong, I suddenly felt waves of approval emanating from what I can only describe as Matilda's presence. On another occasion when Nancy and I had a blazing row, in the aftermath of this I felt waves of disapproval from the same source. It did seem that Matilda was a woman who liked an orderly, harmonious household.

One night I woke up in the early hours and the curtain hanging in the doorway of the dining room had been left open and for one split second I could have sworn I saw Matilda sat in a chair facing the doorway. These visitations and feelings of her presence continued throughout my stay in the house, although they subtly changed as time went on. At first I was frightened when I thought I had caught sight of Matilda or when I sensed her presence, but as the weeks progressed, these episodes no longer worried me, instead they just felt familiar and non-threatening. I am aware that these phenomena can be explained as the imaginings of an overactive mind. I had recently moved into a strange house in a strange country, it was quite understandable. It certainly did not feel as though I was imagining it at the time though. All very strange.

*

Life at the little house got into a routine. Kate cooked, I cleared up, we both cleaned and tidied, and Nancy generally made a mess and went out a lot. She had hired a scooter from Rakmir on her arrival in Goa and having visited the area on several occasions previously, she was quite au fait with the place and always off somewhere, doing something. She had arranged for us to have a market stall at the Saturday Night Market in Arpora, but this had not started yet and there was no date forthcoming off the management. She had also booked us a stall on the Wednesday Flea Market in Anjuna and this was to start the week after Kate's departure for home.

Nancy suddenly became anxious about the stock for the market stall. She had designed and arranged for the manufacture of ten handbags in Mumbai and we had brought these with us to Goa. She had also designed and organised for five different artworks to be screen printed as postcards; one hundred of each. They were elaborate designs of elephants, birds, and flowers printed in gold and black ink on thick, natural card; quite beautiful. So now we started to work on making jewellery from the beads and gems we had purchased in Mumbai. It was quite a little cottage industry that we got going; we would all sit together in the dining room with music playing, chatting and laughing whilst making our designs. It was interesting to see how we all had such different styles. I tended towards quick and easy to make chunky pieces, such as bag charms and key ring fobs. Nancy tended towards intricate, delicate, time consuming pieces, such as cut through leather earrings and brooches; they were beautiful and elegant but slow to produce. Kate was more experimental, fiddling with large stones and pieces of wire, but never quite finishing anything. Slowly our jewellery stock took shape and by the end of the first week in the house together we had quite a collection.

We were busy and occupied with our cottage industry and although we would dine out at least once a day sometimes at lunchtime, but mostly in the evening, we had not had a night out, whereby we went dancing and drinking, since our arrival in India. So we decided to remedy this and arranged to visit Curly's Bar in Anjuna where they were holding a party a couple of days before Kate was due to leave to go back home. It was exciting getting dressed up to go out and we all argued over using the one small mirror we possessed which was hung on the dining room wall. We swapped clothes and jewellery aiming for the perfect ensemble and all admired each other as we waited for Rakmir to arrive with the rickshaw to take us into town. On arrival at Curly's, which was a beach bar, we were greeted with the music blasting out. It was a genre of music I would become all too familiar with over the next few months — Goan Trance. For those not in the know, trance music is a repetitive booming sound with a loud bass and little variance to the melody, apart from the odd random word thrown in for good measure. It was played at such a level that it made normal thought processes nigh on impossible.

Presumably in a bid to deter misbehaviour, licensing laws in Goa allow premises to be open only until ten o'clock at night. Although the bars and clubs applied for late licenses, these were limited, resulting in each evening only one bar in a town would be granted a license for a party. Local Goan women would arrive at the beach outside of the designated bar just before sunset, and with lightning speed they would set up tables and lay mats on the beach. They lit kerosene lamps and sold the most delicious omelettes cooked on little camping gas stoves. They also sold chai the sweet Indian tea, chewing gum, chocolate, cigarettes, cigarette papers, tobacco, and water. In short everything a party reveller could possibly need. Other Goans would arrive to peddle jasmine flower necklaces, torches, laser lights, and LED balls which bounced metres high into the air. With hordes of people congregating on the beach and bar to dance and chat and with music blaring and laser lights piercing the black sky, a party atmosphere was guaranteed.

That night was no different and after going to the bar and braving the music for a short while, we went over to one of the omelette sellers on the beach that was far enough away from the bar so that we could talk. We bought omelettes and chai and sat down on the mats to eat and drink. It was good to people watch, with all sorts of crazy action going on around us. Lots of people were dancing in the sand and the sea, some obviously more aware of reality than others. The drug culture in Goa is rife. Somebody next to me passed a joint and feeling in the party mood I inhaled it trying not to cough. I passed it on to Kate. This seemed to be a pattern throughout the evening and everything became blurry around the edges and difficult to remember as the night wore on.

At around two in the morning, the three of us walked down the beach in the dark towards the town. We were laughing and happy with our arms around each other, the camaraderie of drugs and drink. We walked into town and waited for a taxi to take us home. In the taxi the atmosphere changed and we became quiet staring out of the windows. Kate and I sat in the back of the taxi and Nancy in the front next to the driver.

"We're going in the wrong direction." Kate suddenly announced. "This isn't the way to Arpora."

I looked out of the window, I had no idea if it was the right direction or not, I still had not got my bearings in the area. I felt panic rise within me though, suppose we were being kidnapped. The taxi driver said nothing he was obviously used to reality-removed foreigners.

"Yes it is," Nancy piped up, "see there's the bridge we cross."

"It's a different bridge," retorted Kate.

"No it isn't."

I stared at the bridge, I had no idea if it was familiar or not, I was still panicking.

"You're just paranoid," Nancy added.

I tried to think rationally. "Actually, my bet's on Nancy because she knows the area and we don't." I deduced finally.

"I know the area and we're going in the wrong direction." Kate still insisted.

"I'll sing for us." Nancy said cheerfully. "That will set our minds at rest."

She began to blast out at full pelt her old favourite from childhood, "King of the Swingers" from Jungle Book. The good-natured driver started to laugh and Nancy sang all the way home at full volume, strangely it eased the journey. We all slept in late the following day and woke up with sore heads, feeling very delicate. Nancy remembered nothing of her singing debut when I reminded her of it and I noticed that Kate did not mention the previous evening's infectious paranoia.

A couple of days after this night Kate left for England. She packed in the morning and we sat on the veranda awaiting Rakmir's brother who was driving her to the airport. The Ragamuffin Gang spotted us and came onto the veranda to play. We had a singsong with them which they always enjoyed, especially when we sang the Beatles song, "All you need is love." We only knew the words to the chorus which we had taught the children and we would all sing it together repeatedly, which they loved. Even little Yasmi would join in, singing the words in her lisping baby tones and clapping her little hands in joy. Then the taxi arrived and we all went to wave Kate off — myself, Nancy, and the Ragamuffin Gang. I noticed that Kate had tears in her eyes as she waved goodbye from the back of the taxi.

Chapter 6: Noises in the Night

The house seemed peculiarly quiet in the days after Kate had left and we realised how much she had organised the day-to-day running of the household in terms of shopping, organising meals, and sorting out the day's agenda. Slowly though we readjusted and organised a new routine for ourselves. Since Kate and I had started our travels we had spent the majority of our time together and apart from an odd occasion, I had not spent any time on my own. This was soon to change, however.

Nancy had made several friends in the area already and some of her friends from Mumbai also visited Goa whilst we lived at the little house. Consequently, she was out and about constantly. I hired a scooter after Kate left, but was extremely nervous about using it as I could not seem to get the hang of the accelerator and would automatically pull back on it when trying to slow down as if it were a brake. The first day that I hired it, Nancy and I went out for dinner in the evening and as I parked the bike, I pulled back on the accelerator just as I was stepping off. The bike zoomed into the restaurant wall with me hanging onto it and Nancy screaming, "Let go of the handle!" Although I escaped with only bumps and bruises, it shook me up.

The first few weeks after hiring the scooter I would only use it if I was following Nancy, as I had no idea where I was and was so focused on the traffic that I never seemed to notice any road signs. I was also slow getting my bearings of the locality due to concentrating so much on the road ahead that I did not take notice of the scenery and landmarks around me. This lack of orientation made me anxious. I was a competent car driver at home and had no problem with getting in my car and driving to the other side of the country if need be; this new feeling was alien to me. I began to worry that I was in the early stages of senility, as I just did not seem to be orientating to my surroundings. I could not recall feeling this old, nervous, and incompetent about anything previously. Nancy, although patient at first with my slow driving, started to become irritated with me and would go ahead and not wait for me to catch up with her. On several occasions I lost her altogether which added further to my stress and misery.

It was during this time that Nancy went to an all night party in Anjuna and I was left alone in the house overnight. Since the rat escapade with Kate, I had noticed droppings on the floor and surfaces on occasions and although I had not seen any vermin, it was becoming rather obvious that Kate's first impression had been correct. Nancy left to go to her party around eight o'clock and I sat on the bed in the front room which we now used as a sitting room, surfing the net on Nancy's laptop. Suddenly I heard a scuttling noise above me and looked up to see a rat running along one of the beams. Oh God! There was a half bottle of wine in the fridge which I downed to calm my nerves. I reasoned that the rats would not come into the house itself as long as I made a noise, so I played music full blast all evening. At around two in the morning, when I felt that I was tired enough to sleep,

I went to bed. I kept the music playing, not only to deter the rats from entering the house, but also so that if they did venture into the rooms I would not hear them. What I did not know about could not hurt me.

I was just drifting off to sleep when I heard an almighty banging on the roof above me, so much so, I thought somebody was trying to break into the house. My heart was pounding in my chest and tears sprung to my eyes, I was terrified. The banging continued and it just sounded as though somebody was on the roof above my bed. It was far too heavy a noise to be vermin. The noise moved from directly above me to above the front room of the house and then, whoever it was, began throwing things and smashing them on the path below. Somebody was trying to break into the house by removing the roof tiles. I jumped out of bed, still terrified and ran into the dining room, unlocked the back door, and ran outside. I intended going to knock on Pashkar's door, my neighbour who lived opposite, but suddenly I became overwhelmed with rage. How dare they do this to me, how dare they? I ran to the front of the house to confront the burglar. The lights from a nearby temple dimly illuminated the house and there, sat on top of the veranda roof was a huge monkey. It had cracked the roof tiles with its weight and was idly picking up the pieces of broken clay and throwing them onto the path below. I began to laugh, shaking with emotion. Seeing me, the monkey immediately scampered up the roof and into the branches of an overhanging tree and disappeared into the darkness of the night.

I returned to the house but was far too wired to sleep. Rats and monkeys do not make for peaceful nights. Nancy returned around six in the morning to lay on the bed in the front room fully dressed and fell fast asleep. Her parting words before slumber were, "Turn that music down, Mama, it's deafening," and then she was gone.

*

One day, Nancy came into the house after being on the veranda cuddling Amber our canine friend. It was a common sight to see the two of them lay side by side on the benches outside both fast asleep and cuddled close.

"Do you know, I think that Amber might be pregnant, I'm sure her belly's getting bigger."

"Oh, I wouldn't think so, darling, she's only a youngster, I bet she hasn't come into her first season yet."

Nancy was right though and Amber got bigger and bigger around the belly. She had always been a hungry dog, but now she was desperate for food, scratching at our door constantly and barking outside of the house, only quietening when we fed her. She would eat anything, and if we had no canned pilchards in the house, she was quite happy with bread soaked in milk, rice, raw eggs, or just a bowl of milk. It was about this time that Nancy started letting Amber come into the house, although I was very much against this for several reasons. Firstly, she had fleas and ticks and I did not want the house infested, in particular, my bed. I was already doing battle with the mosquitoes to prevent bites I did not want to add fleas to the list. Secondly, I did not want to get attached to Amber, nor her to us. It was not fair; we were only here for six months and then what would happen to her? Nancy, however, reasoned that it was better that she had six months of love and luxury than none at all and, so, whenever I was not around, Amber was swiftly ensconced into the house and onto Nancy's bed. She loved it.

Some of the neighbourhood children came knocking on our door one day, to ask us if we wanted two puppies. We knew they weren't Amber's as we saw her daily and she was still very pregnant. They brought the two little bundles of fur onto the veranda. The puppies were about six weeks old, we guessed, as they were walking well and had open eyes and could eat independently. We quizzed the children as to where they had come from and apparently they had been found in the fields at the back of the houses a few days ago and the children had taken them home. However, their parents would not let them keep the puppies any longer and had told them to return them to where they had found them. We asked the children about the puppies' mother, but the children insisted that there had not been a dog nearby and they had not seen one around the neighbourhood looking for her pups. It was a mystery.

The puppies were two adorable little boys and we christened them "Pissy Pete" and "Shitty Shaun" for obvious reasons. It seemed that every five minutes they left a puddle or a mess to be cleared up. We could not let the children take the puppies back to the field to be abandoned and so we told them that we would keep them for a few days whilst we tried to find the mother or the owner. We put the little puppies in a basket and they lay there quite peacefully, however, it was obvious that they were not very well. Although adorable, their coats and eyes were dull and their little bellies swollen, we suspected, with worms. They should have been adventurous and full of mischief but, instead, they were tired and listless. We decided to keep them overnight, feed and water them and then take them to a local animal rescue centre in the morning. They did eat a little food and have a few drinks but mostly they lay in the basket either sleeping or excreting. In the morning we took a taxi to the rescue centre and dropped off the puppies. I felt mean and sad.

"They'll probably put them down," Nancy reasoned.

"I know, but would you rather they starved to death on the streets? At least it's quick and painless."

We were silent in the taxi ride home. Life can seem so cruel and pointless sometimes.

Amber also had her puppies, five in total the children informed us. We knew she was due any moment as she was large and eating whatever she could forage. She was anxious too, desperate to come into our house to nest, but I had forbidden this, as I did not want to be responsible for a dog and her puppies, knowing that we were leaving the country in a few months. This was just not our problem and I did not want to be involved. Nancy for once agreed, it was one thing leaving Amber to fend for herself again once we had left, but entirely another letting defenceless puppies fend for themselves, Pete and Shaun had demonstrated this to us quite clearly. So the last few days before the birth we had not seen so much of Amber. She would come to the house scratching at our front door then gulp down the pilchards we gave her, slurp some water, wag her tail, and hare off again, goodness knows where.

The children had seen her coming out of a small hole under one of the houses and guessed that this was where she had made her den. They watched the hole closely for a few days and then one day Amber appeared with a puppy in her mouth. She went tearing off with the puppy and came back in a few minutes for another one, she did this five times. She was on the move apparently. At this time she would come tearing to the house, full of anxiety, gulp down whatever food we gave her, and then tear off again. Motherhood was an anxious time for Amber. She began to smell quite badly and we suspected that she had a uterine infection as she kept licking her rear end. I was quite worried about her and kept wondering how we could get her to see a vet when we did not know where the puppies were or how she would take to coming in a taxi with us. She was dreadfully thin at this time as she was feeding the puppies, which added to my anxiety about her. However, she did pick up and calm down and although we never did get to see the puppies, we did see Amber return to her former self; happy and looking healthy.

*

This first month when Nancy and I lived together was the most stressful for me. I could not relax at home after seeing the rat and I could not relax when going out because of my anxiety about riding the scooter. I was beginning to wonder whatever I was doing in India and started to contemplate returning home early. With hindsight I can see that this was an adjustment period; I had left everything familiar to me and was encountering new challenges constantly. I was in overload and knew that something had to give. I felt lonely; I did not have any friends in the area and was relying on Nancy for companionship and socialisation. It was not fair on her to have to take her mother everywhere with her and I was acutely aware that I was becoming a burden. I had to get myself together and quickly. I thought about why I could not orientate myself to the geography of the area and I realised that I did not take my eyes off the road long enough to notice landmarks because I was too busy looking for traffic and keeping up with Nancy who was always ahead of me. I had to start going out on my own and I had to start looking around me when I rode.

Apart from the problem acclimatising to the accelerator on the scooter was the issue of the traffic in Goa. Health and safety are not awarded the same importance in India as in Britain and very few riders (including myself) wore either padded clothing or helmets due to the heat. There did not appear to be any particular traffic rules, and basically it was a free-for-all on the roads. Cars would pull out of side streets onto main roads with no regard for oncoming traffic, the use of indicators was almost non-existent, overtaking on blind bends seemed to be a national pastime, and driving with full beam on at night regardless of oncoming traffic was de rigueur! The only common rule that seemed to apply was the use of the horn, which had quite a different connotation here to when used in Britain. In Goa, the horn was used to inform other drivers that you were there, so when pulling out of a junction onto a main road, drivers would merrily blast their horns at the oncoming traffic warning them to give way. Overtaking on narrow blind bends did not seem to be regarded as problematic as long as the drivers blasted their horns to warn the vulnerable traffic travelling in the opposite direction. Trust and a deity of choice on the dashboard appeared to give faith that the approaching traffic would slow down or stop. Unfortunately, the gods were not always observing and I witnessed several accidents during my time in India. In addition to the unpredictable and downright dangerous drivers were the free-range cows, dogs, and goats that wandered along the roads, walking straight in front of vehicles whenever they chose. It was no wonder I was anxious.

Eventually though I did acclimatise to both the traffic and the scooter and although I never drove fast, I did begin to love riding along with the warm breeze caressing me, admiring the scenery and thanking the universe for all my blessings. Strange how time can alter one's outlook.

*

Both Nancy and I had intended to start yoga classes when we arrived in Goa and had made several inquiries in regard to this, however, they all seemed to be run by visitors to Goa and were quite expensive in comparison to what we paid back home and we were on a tight budget. One day, when we were out on the scooters, we passed a large detached house that had a notice outside declaring that it was an Ashram, the residence of a religious community and its guru, and advertising yoga classes. Nancy flagged me down further up the road and we decided to turn around and call at the Ashram to find out the prices and availability of the classes. We walked around the side of the building where there was a young boy playing and we asked him who we could talk to about the yoga. He spoke English and said to follow him. He led us around the back of the house, through a porch, around some barking dogs, and eventually to an outside pavilion type building, which was obviously where the yoga classes took place. It consisted of a large concrete platform covered in yoga mats and with a canopy of weaved matting overhead to keep off the sun's rays. At the end of the platform was a large white tent, the door was shut. "Here you are," the boy informed us, and went off back towards the house.

Two men were sat on yoga mats in cross-legged positions as though they were waiting for a class to begin. One of the men introduced himself, telling us that he was the owner of the house and had started the Ashram. We asked him about the yoga classes and he informed us that the Baba was coming soon and would answer our questions. In the Hindu religion, Baba is the name given to a Sadhu or holy man who wanders the country and is often a yogi, a practitioner of yoga. The man went on to inform us that at the Ashram, yoga was regarded as a way of life, a spiritual as well as a physical experience and that the Baba would tell us more about this when he arrived, but that the money for the classes was not important, we could pay what we were able. This seemed to be our sort of yoga! He introduced the other man as an expert in Sanskrit devotional singing; the man smiled shyly and said "Hello."

Just then there was a roar of a motorbike and a Norton Royal Enfield Bullet came screaming into the yard and stopped by the concrete platform and off stepped the Baba. He was dressed from head to foot in white robes and was tall and very, very thin. He had long greasy hair that was combed flat across his head and sported a long, straggly grey beard. His age was indeterminable; he could have been anything between 30 and 60. He was vaguely attractive despite the hair, as he had the clearest, piercing brown eyes that I have ever seen. He smiled at us all benevolently, then joining his hands together in prayer he bowed to us muttering "Namaste," the Indian spiritual greeting, and then disappeared into the white tent. Nancy and I looked at each other bemused. The owner of the house followed him, as did the singer and we were left outside wondering what to do. We sat there for a few minutes when the owner popped his head out of the tent and invited us to join them.

The tent was quite large and had cushions on the floor and a sound speaker in the middle. The men were sat around the speaker with the Baba sat on a raised platform at the back of the tent. Two cushions were placed at the left hand side of the Baba and we sat down. We were offered drinks and when we accepted, a bell was rung and a lady, who was introduced to us as the owner's wife, came into the tent to take our order and deliver our drinks.

"We were just wondering how much your yoga classes are?" Nancy ventured once we had the formalities over with.

The Baba raised a hand in protest.

"What are your names?" he asked.

We told him our names.

"Jill and Nancy," he said, "first Baba must chant."

Then he turned towards me.

"Jill," he said, his piercing eyes staring at mine without blinking. "You are welcome to the Baba's Ashram at any time. Please come and sit in the Baba's tent in comfort; bring your books and read. The Baba's home is your home, Jill."

I was flabbergasted and did not know what to say. Was he coming onto me? His remark seemed out of context and rather strange; why not invite both of us? His constant references to himself in the third person gave his speech a strange arrogance. I glanced at Nancy, her eyes opened wide. I managed to mutter "Thank you."

Then Indian music began playing from the speaker in the middle of the room and the Baba began to chant, with the other two men joining in. The chanting went on for around half an hour. I was uncomfortable both physically and emotionally; the floor cushion was thin and the floor beneath concrete, but I also felt embarrassed by the intimacy of the happenings. I dare not look at Nancy for fear we would start giggling. The chanting took the form of a sort of wailing with the man who was the singer going into elaborate falsetto yodels and the Baba joining in with a harmony that sounded flat and off key. Every so often, the Baba would click his fingers and chant "Ommmmmmmmm." After around ten minutes, I suddenly had a thought. This was the spiritual side of India that I had come to find and here I was feeling embarrassed and imagining that the holy man was being lecherous. I felt ashamed of myself. Just because I did not understand this religion or culture did not mean that I could not embrace it. I tried very hard to sit and listen to the chanting without being judgemental or feeling self-conscious.

After around half an hour the music stopped. The owner of the house announced that now the Baba would talk to us. I noticed that he was very reverent in the way he addressed the holy man, obviously placing him in high esteem. The Baba turned towards Nancy and me.

"To you I am Baba, but Baba is also a man. Baba digs in the garden, Baba tends to the flowers, you say 'Baba, oh Baba,' but I say to you Baba is also a man."

68

He then clicked his fingers and stared at us unblinkingly for several minutes. Again it was an uncomfortable experience and, again, my western sensibilities were screaming at me that this man had a rather large, uncontrolled ego; but I kept squashing these irreverent thoughts telling myself that this was the spiritual side of India that I had so yearned for.

The Baba gave us several more pearls of his wisdom ending with what he referred to as his philosophy.

"Baba's philosophy to life is this. You hold up a glass of water and say that this water consists of hydrogen and oxygen atoms, the glass is made from heating sand and chemical reactions, but Baba say 'No.' This is a glass of water from the tap for a thirsty man." He clicked his fingers and stared at us in a self-satisfied manner. We nodded and smiled vaguely. We were then given leaflets for the yoga classes and told to return at seven thirty in the morning for our first class.

"Jill," the Baba addressed me just as I was leaving the tent, "don't forget, you are welcome to Baba's Ashram at any time."

Nancy and I left the tent in silence and walked to the front of the house.

"Well, that was trippy!" Nancy said at last. "What did you make of it?"

"Well, I didn't really understand what was going on, but I'm trying very hard to be non-judgemental about it." I replied. "They were very welcoming and generous and I think we're seeing it from a western view-point — in ignorance really."

"Mmmm," Nancy replied unconvinced.

As it was we overslept in the morning and missed the class and somehow life took over and we didn't make the class the next day either or the next week.

One Friday evening, a couple of weeks after our visit to the Ashram, Nancy announced that she was going to a party at Hilltop, a rave venue near to Vagator town. She was meeting a few people there and invited me to come along. Never wanting to stay in the house alone in the evenings, I accepted her offer. We rode to the venue on our bikes, about a half hour's ride away. We met up with Nancy's friends and had a dance to the trance music that was playing, but I was not really in the mood for trance and wandered off to explore the venue. The grounds of Hilltop were huge, a large area, about the size of a football field on top of a hill, with a stage in the middle where the dancers congregated in a tight pack. The bar was against the back wall of the venue and, around the sides, the omelette ladies had set up camp, much as they did for the beach parties; laying down mats and lighting kerosene lamps, cooking omelettes and making chai on portable gas stoves. Customers sat on the mats chatting and playing guitars and drums. In other parts of the venue, people were juggling with fire sticks and LED poi sticks or hula hooping. I wandered around for a little while and then bought a cup of chai and sat down on a mat to people watch. There were about a thousand people at the venue, although it could easily have held ten times that number. As I was looking around, I noticed that the Baba we had met at the Ashram was sat on the floor at the next omelette seller's stall to mine, playing a sitar to a small crowd of people. I finished my chai and wandered over to greet him.

By the time I had arrived he was sitting alone as the small crowd had dispersed when he stopped playing and had gone elsewhere to watch other attractions. I tapped him on the arm and said "Hello," warmly. His eyes lit up.

"Come and walk with Baba," he invited me.

I agreed and walked around the venue with him. I apologised for not attending his yoga classes explaining that I was not good at getting up early in the mornings and would be better attending a later class. He smiled generously.

"Baba feel the connection between us when you touched Baba," he said. "Baba is a baba, but Baba is also a man," he continued. "Baba find you very attractive and Baba is big Baba, Baba last long time. Baba give much pleasure and Baba teach you non-attachment." He clicked his fingers.

I should have been shocked by his outburst, but somehow, within the safety of the venue, I found the whole situation hilarious. So much for my spiritual India. We sat down on some chairs and he continued for a while in a similar vein.

"But, Baba," I insisted, "I like attachment."

"No, no, attachment no good," he said, "Baba teach you this and anyway Baba need a helper, you can take yoga classes for Baba, Baba tired of taking yoga. Baba need a woman, Baba big Baba, Baba last long time. We can work together, Baba show you. You can stay with Baba at Ashram." He clicked his fingers. He was hugely comical, one great big egocentric letch. Just then two of Nancy's friends sat on the chairs next to us. They leant over to say "Hello," to me, so I introduced Baba to them. He quickly whispered in my ear.

71

"This talk is between you and Baba, not to tell other people what Baba say."

He leant over and shook their hands giving them his finest intense stare. By then I had well and truly got the measure of Baba and was looking around to find Nancy, I spotted her with her friend Emma.

"I must go," I announced, "my daughter Nancy is waiting for me."

He turned towards me, realisation suddenly dawning on his face.

"You came to Baba's Ashram," he said. "You came with your daughter, a few weeks ago."

"Yes," I agreed, "that was me."

The letch had not even recognised me. The fact that I had touched his arm and said "Hello," was enough for him to invite me to have sex and teach yoga for him. I told Nancy and Emma what had happened, they were shocked.

"Oh my God, I don't believe it," Nancy said. "The slime ball."

After that evening another catch phrase was born in our little house to be used whenever we selfishly wanted something.

"Mama, are you making a brew?"

"No, Nancy, I've made it the last few times, it's your turn, madam!"

"But, Mamaaaaa, Baba big Baba, Baba last long time!"

Chapter 7: Market Traders

With the material that Nancy had brought with her from Mumbai, we decided to make some waistcoats to sell on the market stalls. Nancy cut a pattern off a waistcoat she already owned and we started a production line; I cut the gorgeous embroidered cloth from the pattern and Nancy sewed them together, then I pressed them. In total we made five reversible waistcoats which were beautiful. We then had the brainwave to make bunting to hang around our stalls so that we would stand out from the crowd. Within the bags of materials was some striped sateen cotton of various colour-ways. Nancy, who I discovered was something of a perfectionist, insisted that the all of the sateen pieces be ironed, then matched and blended for aesthetic appeal. We cut out hundreds of triangles from a template, tacked and sewed two pieces together so that the bunting was lined, turned them right side out, pressed them all, colour matched them again, and then sewed them onto black ribbon. We made four separate strings of ten feet, with loops of ribbon sewn onto each end in order to hang them around the four sides of the stalls. Never was there such smart bunting.

We still had no idea when the Saturday Night Market was starting, but the Wednesday Flea Market was in full swing when we arrived in Goa and our first market there was the week after Kate had left. That morning we set our alarm for six o'clock, both took showers that immediately woke us up, and got dressed. We had planned our outfits the night before, funky market traders was the look we were going for. We both wore one of the waistcoats we had made, as walking adverts for our stall. We loaded our scooters precariously piled high, Indian style, with two plastic chairs to sit on; the old wooden table from the house; an old fashioned suitcase Nancy had found in her flat in Mumbai which we were going to use as a display case, three carved wooden frames which we had backed with material to display the jewellery we had made, a plastic stool to place the case on, and a large bag which contained the goods we were selling. We strapped the load to our bikes with bungee ropes, there was hardly any room left for us to sit on the scooters and then we set off in tangent to the market which was in Anjuna by the beach.

The Indian man, Anthony, who managed the market, had taken a shine to Nancy. He was apparently renowned for his attraction to the prettier, younger market trader, and he had given us a stall near to the main bar on a busy thoroughfare, it was a good spot. We carried our wares from the car park to the stall and set up the old wooden table and sat the retro suitcase open on the plastic stool to display our goods. We tied bamboo canes to the table legs in order to raise the sides of the table; then we ran string across the two raised canes and balanced the carved picture frames against these to display our jewellery. We placed the postcards Nancy had designed in front of the frames. We put some of the handbags inside the open suitcase and some on the table. The waistcoats we put on hangers and draped off the wooden frames. Then finally, we hung a couple of strings of bunting around the stall and sat down on our chairs at either side to await the custom. Surprisingly, the stall looked good. The old table, retro case, hand carved picture frames, and immaculate bunting blended together perfectly and gave the impression of something from a magazine shoot that a stylist had put together. I was beginning to appreciate my daughter's experience and feel for design. Within the first half hour, we had sold around a dozen of the postcards and a lady from Australia had admired the quality of the material that the waistcoats were made from. We told her the story of how we had acquired the material and she told us that she was also a textile designer. She bought one of the waistcoats. We asked her if she wanted to try it on first, but she declined stating that it did not matter if it fitted or not, as it would always fit somebody and it was the material she was in love with. We had made around 100 pounds in the first hour of trading, this was amazing.

By the end of the day we had also sold one of the handbags and had learnt an awful lot about sales. These were always made when we engaged with the customer in conversation, but this was a delicate act as it could easily frighten potential customers away. We tried various techniques to begin conversation and discovered that the easiest method was to ask people where they had come from, or if they were on holiday, or simply to admire something that the customer was wearing. There was more to this trading lark than we first thought. If the customer was friendly we would then start, what we later came to refer to as our "mother and daughter act." The customer would admire something on the stall, usually a postcard, and I would begin the tale of how Nancy had designed these and how they were screen printed by hand. The customer would say how beautiful they were and I would agree stating that Nancy was extremely talented and had also designed the handbags, which were fabulous too. Nancy would then pipe up and explain in an embarrassed tone that I was her mother. The customers would laugh, but it had hooked them in and they loved the story of how I had taken a career break to come out to India and help my talented daughter set up her dream design business. Seemingly it was perfectly acceptable and quite endearing to others to hear me boast about my daughter's talents.

The first market went well and we were thrilled with our profits. We had decided to plough all of the money we made back into the business and live off our savings. So after each market, once we got home, we would empty our moneybags and count the profits. I used to love doing this, as it always seemed to me miraculous that we could make money from so little an initial investment. In truth, we paid for the market stalls from our own money and, with hindsight, I realise that there was no way that we could have lived in India with the money we earned from trading. It was just too expensive to hire a stall and we were not selling enough goods. We barely broke even. However, because we funded the stalls from our own funds and because we took no salaries, we were able, over the course of the six months, to have quite a few more of Nancy's handbag designs made up. We sourced a tailor in Baga, a nearby town, who produced work to Nancy's perfectionist standard. The ethos of MamaNoo was high quality products, Nancy had insisted upon this.

The other market traders on the day market were a mixture of Indians selling traditional wares and other western designers selling jewellery and clothing. The Indian traders were hard line sellers, haggling with the customers and not letting them walk away without looking at their stalls. One of the younger traders was renowned for chasing after every customer with a better offer if they walked away empty-handed. It was reported that he was one of the best sellers on the market. The traders were all friendly and would help one another by covering the stalls whilst a trader went to the toilet or to buy food. The stallholders would tie saris above the stalls to provide shade from the glaring sun and would help one another to move the saris along as the sun moved across the sky. The trader at the back of us, an Indian man selling traditional metal ornaments, would howl laughing at us every week as we tied bamboo and string to our tatty old table Heath Robinson style and hung up our bunting. He did not understand the old fashioned look we were aspiring to with our stall design and, obviously, to him it just looked like old junk that we were displaying our wares on. He was a lovely, warm, friendly man however, and would make a point of tying his sari up so that it covered our stall too and would often give us tips on engaging our customers in conversation. It was hard to believe that this gentle, friendly man could suddenly turn into a hardnosed salesman as soon as a holidaymaker walked within 20 yards of his stall. He would arrive at six o'clock in the morning to set up and not start packing up until around seven o'clock at night. He worked six days a week he told us, this was his living and he had a wife and children to feed. What we were playing at was the livelihoods of these market traders. It was a battle out there and they were in it to win it.

*

A reoccurring clash happened regularly with Nancy and me over her constant habit of losing things; her keys, her phone, her purse, and even her handbag on one occasion. It was almost every time we went out together that she would leave something at a venue or not be able to find her scooter keys, or leave her phone lying somewhere only to find it had disappeared. The six months we were in India she permanently lost two phones, two keys to MamaNoo house, her handbag, and her purse, which meant that she had no credit card and for the rest of our time in India I was tasked with withdrawing money for her that she then transferred back into my bank. She never did phone her bank to report the card lost or to request a replacement. Her absentmindedness also affected other people, it was a nuisance. We would arrange to go out and Nancy would spend half an hour looking for her scooter keys, dragging anyone who was around into the drama. I wondered if for some reason it only happened when I was there, but her friends assured me otherwise. It was like a disability, it was so pronounced. I tried to discuss tactics for memory improvement with her, but she would fly off the handle when I raised the topic, becoming defensive to what she perceived as criticism. "You forget things too," she screamed at me one day when I raised the topic again, whilst she was throwing stuff about the house manically looking for her scooter keys. It was to be a prophetic statement.

78

The next Wednesday, Nancy and I decided to arrive at the market stall early in the morning, as we had been late for the last few weeks and were trying to make amends. We drove in convoy to the market, our scooters loaded up with goods, as always. We parked in the little car park that we had found, away from the larger, sprawling car park that the tourists used. We were chatting as I unlocked the seat of my scooter that housed a storage compartment also filled with goods. We walked to the market stall laden up and spent our usual 12 hours at the market. Once it got dark, around seven that evening, we packed up the stall and I went into my moneybag to remove my scooter keys, but no keys were there. I panicked and ran to the car park whilst Nancy watched over the goods back at the stall. It was dark, but I could clearly see Nancy's scooter parked on its own. In disbelief I ran round and round the car park, but my scooter was not in hiding anywhere. I had left the keys in the seat of my scooter and somebody had stolen it. I walked back to the stall crying at my own stupidity. Nancy was totally supportive, "Don't worry, Mama, we'll sort it. It will all be all right. You'll see." There was no way we could get a taxi to take me home at that time, the market was heaving.

"Let's load up my scooter and then see if we can get you a lift back with somebody. You take this suitcase and bag with you." Nancy suggested.

"What about the police," I wondered. "Shouldn't we be phoning the police?"

"I think we better call Rakmir first and check; he shouldn't be renting out scooters without a licence. He'll get into trouble."

We decided to wait until I got home before phoning Rakmir and facing his predictable wrath.

We walked over to some Indian men and women who were loading up a large open truck. We explained that my scooter had been stolen and asked if they were going anywhere near to Arpora and could they give me a lift. They willingly obliged. So I sat on top of their goods on the back of the truck along with about six other women stallholders, who smiled at me sympathetically. They dropped me near to MamaNoo House and I phoned Nancy and she collected me on her scooter, having already reached home and unloaded the goods. There is a definite advantage of transport by scooter on market day as they can weave in and out of the queues of traffic travelling along the dirt track that leads to the market. We phoned Rakmir and he was furious, coming round to the house immediately to discuss the matter. We omitted to say that the keys had been left in the seat of the scooter. When he demanded where the keys to the scooter were I, truthfully, explained that at the end of the day I had discovered that they were missing from my moneybag where I always kept them. He jumped to the conclusion that somebody had watched me arrive and stolen the keys from my bag. He was raging and then bluntly stated, "You will have to pay for the scooter, of course." Nancy, very calmly, explained that we did not have money to pay for a scooter, but that we would notify the police to see what they could do about it. He calmed down, noticeably, asking us not to contact the police. It was his Achilles heel and we kicked it hard. Every time he mentioned money, we discussed phoning the police. In the end he left, saying that he would search for the bike and cautioned us, again, not to phone the police.

We went out for dinner that evening and explained to friends what had happened, again omitting to tell that the keys had been left in the bike, as we did not want this related back to our young friend. Everybody told us that we would be asked to pay for the bike and everyone advised us not to hand over any money, stating that the owners would claim it back on insurance. I felt better about my stance after this, although I was still feeling guilty and worried. The next day Rakmir turned up at the house triumphant, he had found the bike. It had been parked down a dirt track near to Vagator, goodness knows how he had found it he must have been searching night and day. We asked him if he tackled the thief, but he said "No," he just rode it away with his spare keys. After that, when parking my scooter, I used the same memory techniques that I had superiorly suggested to Nancy may help her and never again forgot my keys.

One evening, after a successful day at the market in which we sold three handbags, we decided to treat ourselves by visiting an expensive Italian restaurant that we had seen. We were always hungry after market day and would not get back to the house until around eight o'clock in the evening, due to the slow traffic leaving the market and the roads being busy with traders. Usually we quickly unloaded our scooters and would then go straight back out, tired and unwashed, to a local restaurant for some food. This evening however, we jumped under the shower to freshen up and got changed into party clothes as this was a definite treat. It was worth the effort as the food and ambiance at the venue was perfect and we celebrated our successful day at the market with three courses and a bottle of wine.

We were brimming with bonhomie when we arrived back home, it had been a particularly successful day and the celebratory meal had been magnificent and culminated with us planning the future of the business. Life was good. This was short lived however, as Nancy upon entering the back bedroom where she now slept began to scream at the top of her voice. She came running into my room.

"Oh my God there was the most enormous rat sniffing around in the corner. It just ran straight up the ladder and into the beams. Urgh!"

Now to give Nancy her due, she was not normally wimpy about either vermin or insects and usually took these in her stride when she encountered them, unlike myself. So for this rat to have frightened Nancy, meant it must have been of some size. This was not reassuring for me.

"I wonder what it was doing in the corner?" I mused.

We were always so careful not to leave food or crumbs lying around as we did not want to encourage these visits.

"I don't know, that's what I was wondering." Nancy replied. "Come on, let's go and have a look."

We walked back into the bedroom and, there in the corner, glaring at us menacingly, was the most enormous spider I have ever seen. I had heard of deadly spiders in India and I was sure that this was one of them. Not only was it huge, but also it was squaring up to us.

"Oh my goodness!" I cried.

Nancy had gone all girly, girly again and was running on the spot.

"Kill it, Mama, kill it," she was shouting.

"I can't kill it, it would take a shot gun to kill that thing." I said. It was still glaring at us, obviously debating whether to attack or flee. It had some guts, that was for sure. It became obvious that Nancy was not going anywhere near this monster, so I was going to have to deal with it alone.

"We're going to have to catch it in something and put it outside. Go and get me a big dish from the kitchen please."

Nancy gratefully ran off whilst the beast and I sparred around each other, gazes never leaving the opponent. She came back with a large plastic container.

"Mmmmm, that will do." I muttered.

I steeled myself to capture it, if it stung me I would be dead, I was pretty sure of that.

As I approached it slowly, it continued to glare at me and then, in the blink of an eye, it turned about and scurried into a hole in the floor that was designed to let the monsoon rains escape. Nancy brought the torch whilst I kept guard and we shone it into the hole. Its eyes, illuminated in the light, were winking at us! We stuffed the hole tightly with paper and looked at each other with relief.

"Let's go and get drunk." Nancy suggested.

It was the only sensible solution really and I readily agreed. This house for all its suburban authenticity was beginning to wear a little thin of late.

Nancy, Mangy Dog, and one of the members of the Ragamuffin children on the veranda of the MamaNoo House.

Nancy and me in the MamaNoo house just about to go out for dinner

Amber and Mangy Dog on the veranda of the house

Little Fred the Voyeur, on the bathroom wall

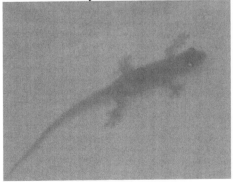

Me on the coach ride from Hell — Bangalore to Goa

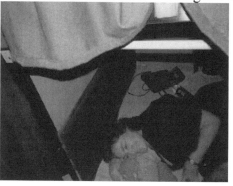

Nancy on the coach — opposite aisle

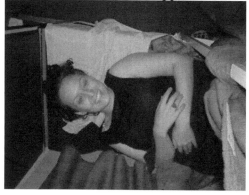

Nestled Amongst Temples

Nancy and me in Mapsa for Holi

Nancy at the MamaNoo stall in Arpora night market, Goa

Nancy sitting on 'the chair' at the night market, Goa

Stood in front of the MamaNoo stall the Saturday Night Market, Arpora, Goa

Nestled Amongst Temples

Photoshoot for MamaNoo handbags, Anjuna, Goa

One of Nancy's art cards — Fatima's Hand

Face painted for a catalogue of face painting styles —
Saturday Night Market, Goa.

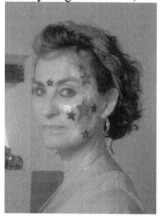

Nancy with face painted for a catalogue of face painting
styles — Saturday Night Market, Goa.

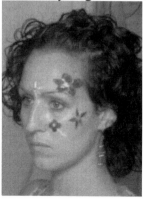

Nestled Amongst Temples

The German Bakery — next door to Nancy's new apartment

Chapter 8: Unwanted Admiration

Not only had we been awarded a prestigious stall at the flea market, one that was on the main walkway to the bar and restaurant, but also we had not been charged any rent there. Anthony, the owner of the bar where the market was held, was a frequent visitor to our stall and obviously enamoured with Nancy. He was about 50 years of age, overweight, and out of shape; the whites of his eyes were a dark yellow. He wore a leery grin on his face and had the Indian habit of shaking his head from side to side constantly when listening to the other person reply when in conversation, his breath always smelled of drink. It never ceased to amaze me why he imagined that my beautiful young daughter would take a second glance in his direction. To make matters worse, his wife and son worked at the bar and could clearly see our stall and its visitors from that vantage point. His wife gave us dark looks whenever we glanced in her direction. They had obviously been an attractive couple in their prime, but he had taken to drink and she had the anger of life's disappointments etched into her face and eyes. The bar and market provided them with a comfortable living and they stayed together for convenience, but there was little love lost between them it seemed. It was rumoured that Anthony constantly pursued young women, which was not too difficult to imagine having seen him in action around my daughter.

Nancy forbade me from warning him not to hassle her, stating that she would handle this herself. After all her hard work and dreams, she did not want to lose the market stall because of some drunken admirer. I found his behaviour completely disrespectful, not only to Nancy, but also to myself. I was her mother, and he was a middle aged, married man, who was obviously trying to coax my daughter into an affair with him in front of my nose. It was extremely difficult for me to stay civil with him as he smarmed around Nancy, constantly showing off and bragging. He was abhorrent. Every week, she offered him the rent we owed, but he would not take it, making a big show of refusing it. Many of the Indian market traders were frightened of him, as it was reported that he had a ferocious temper and on a whim would ban people from the market and, thus, their livelihood.

A much larger stall than ours had recently become vacant nearby, on the same row, and we had been considering asking Anthony if we could move into this, but it was a difficult situation as we had not paid any rent so far and did not feel that we were in a position to request favours. He would regularly phone Nancy to ask her to go out with him, but she always acted as though he were asking simply out of friendship and pleasantly refused in a matter-of-fact way, stating that she had already made arrangements for the particular evening in question. He phoned one day to ask if she wanted to go to a party at a bar nearby to his, but she thanked him and said that she was going out to dinner with me, so he extended the invitation to me also. For once, Nancy agreed to go, as she felt that it might be the bargaining tool she needed to request a change of stall to the larger, more prestigious position. I felt unsure about this, warning her that he could easily misconstrue her acceptance of the invitation, whether or not her mother was chaperoning her.

We arrived at the bar in question and were soon joined by Anthony, who ordered drinks and an array of dishes to be brought to our table. The food was superb, as this particular bar was renowned for its cuisine, especially its signature dishes of freshly caught seafood and fish. He insisted that we both try the calamari, telling us that it was not like the usual calamari at all. He was right, it was divine, unlike anything that I had tasted before, crispy on the outside but soft and delicious inside, it almost melted in the mouth. It was mouth watering. A live band was playing reggae music and the place soon became packed with people, eating and drinking. Anthony ensured that the drinks flowed all evening. We were both enjoying ourselves and I rather naively found myself wondering if he was rather lonely and just wanted the company of women and did not really want anything more. I should have known that there is no such thing as a free meal.

Nancy and I had been dancing on the small dance floor in front of the stage when she left to go to the toilet. I wandered back to the table for a drink and discovered that Anthony was no longer there either. Nancy was gone for a while and, as I was beginning to get anxious, I walked towards the toilets, which were outside at the back of the bar, to look for her. As I walked outside, she was coming inside, we collided.

"Let's get out of here, Mama," she announced. "That creep has just tried it on with me."

"Let's pay for our food and drink first," I said, "and then we don't owe him anything." We went to the bar to pay, but when the girl asked us what table we were sat at, she announced there was no charge as that was Anthony's table and he did not pay. It was obviously some arrangement that the bar owners had between themselves, and so we quickly left; Nancy telling me what had happened as we walked into town to get a taxi. Apparently, as she was leaving the toilet, Anthony was standing in the courtyard outside talking to the bar owner. He called her over, put his arm around her shoulder and introduced her as his girlfriend. Nancy protested, saying that she was not his girlfriend, but just a friend. The restaurant owner had started laughing and Anthony, obviously embarrassed by Nancy's denial and feeling that he was losing face in front of his friend, had pushed Nancy against the wall and started to kiss her. She pushed him away, whereby he had snarled at her that she better comply or she need not come back to the market again. She walked off with him shouting after her that he knew people and could easily have her thrown into jail if he wanted to.

"So where does this leave us for next week?" I asked. "We can't go back to the market now, he'll throw us out."

"We certainly can, Mama. I've done nothing wrong, besides, if he throws us out then everyone will know exactly why. I don't think he'll do anything. He's a big coward."

So the next week we turned up at the market, as usual, and Nancy was right, we did not get thrown out. In fact, we did not see Anthony at all during the day, and that was not the only thing that was different. When his heavies, two thick-set brusque, unsmiling men, came around collecting the stallholders' rents, they did not walk straight past our stall as they usually did, but this week they stopped and menacingly demanded the rent. We paid up and one of the men carefully put a tick against our stall number in the accounts book he was holding, which had previously contained just a row of blanks. Times were, obviously, a changing.

*

We saw Anthony again at the markets that followed, but he was no longer friendly towards us and did not stop to chat as he had in the past. He no longer phoned Nancy and, in all, it made life a lot easier. Rumour on the market was that he had gone on the wagon again, a regular occurrence apparently and one that turned his leery grin to a frown. Apparently, the grape vine informed us, he became more aggressive when sober and took to hitting the waiters and banning more stallholders from his market. One Wednesday, we saw him walking down our aisle, stopping and talking to certain stallholders, he stopped at our stall to invite us to his son's birthday party at the bar the following Saturday, it was to celebrate his 21st birthday. He asked us in an indifferent tone, neither smiling nor frowning simply adding the time to arrive and then moving on. As some of the other stallholders we knew were attending, we decided to go. It might help to move the relationship into an easier space.

We arrived on our scooters the following Saturday and the bar and outside area, where the market stalls were usually spread out, had been completely transformed. There were streams of white fairy lights hanging everywhere, and a bamboo arch had been placed in the sand near to the bar entrance for people to enter through, this had also been covered in lights. The tables and chairs from the bar had been placed outside under the fairy lights where the stalls normally were, it looked unrecognisable. The bar had been emptied apart from two long trestle tables that were loaded with food, with waiters standing behind these to serve guests. Outside of the bar was an open dance tent with a raised platform on which four members of a band were stood playing popular western songs. We quickly spotted our friends and joined their table, an elderly waiter whom we knew from being served at the bar on a Wednesday came over to take our order. There was no charge for the drinks. In all, the venue and food had been laid out to cater for around 100 people, there were about 30 people there, when we arrived, fashionably late at half past eight. We went over to Sebastian to wish him a happy birthday and to give him the card and present that we had bought for him. This was the first time we had ever spoken to him, so we explained who we were. He thanked us politely.

The atmosphere at the party was dead. Although the music was playing loudly, nobody was dancing and with all the empty tables and chairs it felt as though it was nearing the end of the evening. After we had been to the buffet, which was plentiful and had hardly been dented we noticed, somebody at our table suggested we dance to liven up the night. So we all stood up and went over to the dance tent for a boogie. Not long after that, other people joined us on the dance floor and the atmosphere livened up somewhat. Throughout the evening, Anthony sat at a table with his wife and some other Indian people. Neither husband nor wife were talking, but both sat, gazes down, glaring into their glasses, of which Anthony's, I noticed, contained orange juice. Near to ten o'clock, Anthony came over to the band and stopped the music, then taking the microphone he thanked us all for coming to the party, telling us what a wonderful son Sebastian was. He then asked us to join in the Lord's Prayer to thank God for all his blessings. He had certainly not struck me as a religious man, but on reflection, it figured. It was a bizarre end to a birthday party.

As soon as the speech was finished, waiters descended on the tables to clear away the glasses and plates, it was clearly the end of the evening. The elderly waiter who had served us previously came up to collect our glasses, mine was still half full.

"I won't be a minute," I told him, taking a swig from the glass.

He smiled at me then whispered conspiratorially, "Please can you hide it under the table, madam, the bar is now shut." Just at that moment, Anthony rushed over to our table and shouted at me to put the drink down and get out. He shoved the waiter in his chest, sending him reeling backwards, yelling that he was a clown, whilst snatching my drink off the table. We were shocked. People were still milling around getting ready to go home and suddenly all eyes were upon our table.

"Get out, get out," he screamed at us, "do you want me to lose my fucking license?" It was totally rude and unnecessary. His bar licence ran until ten o'clock and it was only a few minutes past this, surely drinking up time was allowed within the law. I noticed Sebastian turning his back on his father and walking hurriedly into the bar. An unpleasant end to his 21st birthday. We hurriedly began to stand up as Anthony stormed off and then we turned to our subdued waiter to ask him if he was all right.

"I am leaving here just as soon as I find a job in a bar far away, where he can't find me," he explained. "He beats me and takes his life pain out on me and he will not give me a letter of recommendation for a new job," he continued. "He kicks me and he kicks his dogs. He is not a good man. But I will find a new job and I will be happy. God will look after me," he added optimistically. We all tipped him generously and hugged him goodnight, he smiled gratefully and waved us goodbye and then went back to clearing the tables, throwing the scraps of food to the dogs that lurked in the shadows.

*

Each week, stood outside the grounds of the Wednesday Flea Market was an elephant and its mahout. It was covered in brightly coloured chalk decorations and spent the day having its photograph taken and giving rides to tourists. I loved riding along the roads to the market on my scooter first thing in the morning and overtaking the elephant as it lumbered along the road with the mahout riding high on its back. Only in India, I always thought, and smiled as I remembered my commute to work along the motorways at home. I discovered that there were three elephants in the Anjuna area, I never saw where they were tethered at night, but I regularly saw them during the day outside of the markets and temples, patiently chewing on large stalks of sugar cane, their heads gaily painted with chalk, waiting for the next tourist to come along. I would always shout out to them as I drove past, "Hello, beautiful," having heard the folklore that elephants never forget and hoping that they would learn to recognise my voice. They never acknowledged me though, but just continued slowly chewing on the stalks and patiently awaiting the next command of their mahout. They seemed such huge, majestic, calmly resigned creatures. It was heartbreaking to think that these beautiful animals were hunted and slaughtered for their tusks. What strange, murderous creatures us humans have proved to be.

The market was also visited by the ceremonial cow and its keeper, who led it up and down the market aisles all day, posing for photographs in exchange for rupees. The cow was covered in a gilded, tasselled ceremonial cloth, its horns and tail bandaged with the same gilded cloth and its eyes darkened with black kohl. A huge bell was hung around its neck and as it tottered along on its lacquered hooves, it tolled its own arrival. Likewise, it had a resigned air of endurance about it, as it stopped for yet another photograph with a tourist's arm wrapped around its neck.

Nancy too was fascinated by these animals and in quiet moments at the market, she would take out her sketch pad and continue to draw an intricate pen and ink picture of this ceremonial cow, ready to be screen printed as art cards for next year's collection. We were already selling an art card of a ceremonial elephant that she had drawn; it was our best selling product. We called it the Nelly card.

Animals were such a noticeable part of Goan life; the elephants lumbering along to market, the street dogs and cats who lay in the shade at the sides of the road, the water buffalo grazing in the fields, the small wild black boars that could be glimpsed in the undergrowth, the cows wandering along the beaches and roads, and the little goats with their dangly ears and bobbing tails that also blocked the roads as they trotted freely in small herds. Apparently, when the first hippies arrived in Anjuna in the early 60's they slept in hammocks in the trees and built pig latrines to collect sewerage. They would build outside toilets high on ramps that could be accessed underneath by wild boar; whenever solid matter fell out of the toilet it was devoured by the wild boars who gathered below. Such a delight was this feast, so the stories go, that the boars would honk loudly with disappointment were it only fluid that fell from the bowl above!

Chapter 9: Christmas

As we moved into December, it was hard to believe that Christmas was only a few weeks away. The blazing sunshine belied the season and despite the multitude of paper star lanterns hanging outside of the shops and restaurants, we were not feeling the festive spirit. "Let's decorate the house, Mama," Nancy suggested one day when I was bemoaning a lack of yuletide vibe. It was a good idea and we planned how we could simply and cheaply make the house more festive. One immediate solution was to hang our beautiful stall bunting around the rooms; we had four long pieces, so we hung these in the two main rooms of the house: the front room and the dining room. It immediately cheered the place up and it was simple enough to unhook them to take with us to the markets.

"Let's buy some fairy lights," I suggested. "We can use them afterwards on the market stalls."

"Yes, let's wind them around coconut branches like they do at the Flea Market, that looks really groovy."

"Oooh yes, good idea, Noodle."

"And we can make a holly wreath for the front door, there's a sort of holly bush in the fields at the back."

We suddenly oozed with ideas for making the house more festive, and picked up a pair of scissors and went off to the fields, cutting branches off the holly bush that was there. The leaves were just as prickly as those of its British counterpart, however, they were a paler green and there were no red berries.

"We can paint some of the leaves red and gold," Nancy suggested, ever the designer. "And weave some scraps of red material amongst the branches."

We brought our spoils home and started to weave the branches together, it was a painful affair as both the leaves and the branches had large spikes on them.

"I think we were a little over enthusiastic in our gathering, Noodle, there's loads here"

"Why don't we make two wreaths and give one to Emma, she'll love that."

Emma was one of Nancy's friends who had also befriended me; we had met her within the first few weeks of our arrival in Goa. So that was what we did. It turned out that Nancy was a bit of an expert at making holly wreaths, as she had once worked in a florist's shop during school holidays and had been taught the skill. We wove bright pieces of cloth in between the holly branches and painted a few of the prominent leaves red and gold. Nancy finished off both wreaths with a large red bow at the top and we tied string to them as a hook. They looked fabulous and very professional, the type of wreath that would be priced at over £100 in Harrods store. We were thrilled and ceremoniously tied our large wreath outside of the front door of the house. Within minutes a group of Indian women who were walking past the house had stopped outside of the garden and were staring at the wreath, discussing this amongst themselves. This carried on all afternoon and evening, with different groups of neighbours and passersby stopping to stare. The holly hanging on the door fascinated everybody; it was obviously not an Indian custom. The Ragamuffin Gang soon arrived, shouting hello at us through the dining room window where they could see us sat at the table. We looked up to see them pointing to our front door with puzzled looks on their faces. We never ceased to be a great source of interest and bemusement in our little neighbourhood.

We bought two strings of fairy lights in purple and pink and went scouring the countryside for coconut branches, intending to emulate the extravaganza of the market lights. As soon as it became dark at the Wednesday Flea Market, the main thoroughfare was lit with an array of fairy lights that were twisted into balls, it looked fabulous. During the day, it was possible to see that the lights were wound around a cut branch that had lots of little branches coming off it like a round multi-pronged fork. We asked somebody what tree these were from, and had been told that they were the branches that the coconuts grow from, and are chopped off when the coconuts are harvested. They were quite different from the palm leaves and we would never have guessed the source unless told. Our first port of call in the search for branches was the nearest coconut seller's stall at the side of the road, and there, sure enough, lying with the discarded coconut shells were several of the branches we coveted. We asked the seller if we could take a couple, and he looked at the branches and shrugged, these strange European people were at it again, acting weird.

At home we trimmed the branches until they loosely resembled a ball shape with a hanging stem and then we carefully weaved the fairy lights in and out of the branches. By this time it was quite dark and so we plugged in our two lights and switched off the overhead ones. Geronimo! They looked spectacular and our little front room was transformed into a fairy grotto. We were extremely pleased with ourselves.

The next time we saw Emma, we gave her the holly wreath and she too was delighted with this, squealing her thanks and telling us how clever we were when we told her we had made it. She hugged us affectionately, confessing that she had forgotten it was almost Christmas. It was Emma's second season in Goa and she knew lots of people and places to go. She was very much a party animal, always out and about. She was in her 20's, with a thick mane of long, wavy brown hair and a pretty face. She had a very shapely figure, about a size 16, reminiscent of Marilyn Monroe's sexy curves and was extremely attractive. She turned heads when she walked into rooms. She came from London and spoke confidently with a public school accent. She had previously worked as a stylist for one of the upmarket magazines and knew several minor celebrities. She was also creative, making unusual, striking headwear out of flowers, feathers, jewels, and beads. Her work had been featured in several high-end fashion magazines. She too was intending on getting a stall on the Saturday Night Market to supplement her income. She was romantic in her styling, wearing feminine broderie anglaise gypsy blouses and little flowery skirts. Her creations were also romantic; headdresses of dozens of blood red roses or large peacock feathers and jewels. Quite striking. She had several tattoos on her body, again along a romantic, fantasy theme; Fatima's Hand on her wrist, a feather dream catcher on her leg, and a web of lace on her arm.

Emma rented a house near to the centre of Anjuna where she lived alone. It was situated in a clearing of trees along with a few other houses. It was the old Portuguese style with open rafters like MamaNoo House, with one huge sitting room, a small kitchen and bathroom and large bedroom. She had rented it unfurnished, although it was now tastefully decorated with old carved pieces and huge tapestry wall hangings. The sitting room had settees covered in a multitude of bright cushions and padded throws. They were in fact old wooden sunbeds with the mattresses covered in bright chintz, having the advantage of being perfect put-me-ups for people staying over. Pride of place in the bedroom, was an old, carved wooden four-poster bed with hangings all round of white muslin, which doubled as mosquito netting. Fairy lights were strewn from the rafters. The carved front door opened onto a porch, which, likewise, was strewn with cushions, throws, and fairy lights. All very romantic. It was the perfect little house in the woods, just like in the fairy tales.

Emma was a very sociable and friendly person, easily making and maintaining friends of all ages and backgrounds. She introduced us to lots of people during our time in Goa and Nancy and her became quite close and went out together in the evenings. Emma always ensured that I was also invited, although I often declined. I was torn between not wanting to stay in the house alone and not wanting to be the unwanted guest with my daughter and her friends. It was a tough call. I reached a compromise whereby I would go out with Nancy and friends during the day, but in the evenings I tended to keep this to just weekends only, unless it was Nancy and I going out for dinner or a drink alone. In this way, I did not feel that I was encroaching upon my daughter and her friends too much. Although one of the wonderful things about Goa was that wherever we went, there was a complete mix of age groups from the very old to the very young. I never, in all the time I spent in India, went to a venue where I felt out of place. It was a common sight at the trance raves to see elderly hippies kicking up a storm on the dance floor, with nobody looking twice at them, as this was just the norm. Not only could you comfortably go into any venue, but you could also dance to your heart's content without feeling the least bit self-conscious.

Emma had been involved with a French man the previous season, she told us, but he had cheated on her although she was still in love with him. He had left to spend the season in Nepal and she had not heard from him since. She was hoping that he would return to Anjuna that season and always had one eye on the doorway, I noticed, whenever we were out somewhere. She warned us that he was not the most attractive of men and stated that sometimes she wondered what she saw in him, but that there was just something about him, she confessed. He was much older than Emma and had a daughter of a similar age to her, whom he never saw. I wondered what such a beautiful, personable young woman was doing with somebody who cheated on her and sounded unattractive. It was not an unusual story, of course.

I was out with Nancy and Emma when she met up again with Pierre. We were in a nightclub in Anjuna and had just gone to the bar to get a drink. Emma suddenly turned to us a ghostly pale and whispered, "Oh, God, he's here!" She was shaking. We knew immediately who she meant.

"Where, where," we asked filled with curiosity, but she dare not turn to look.

"Don't look, don't look, let me get myself together," she pleaded. We went outside whilst Emma went through a whole gamut of emotions in a short space of time. Eventually, she pulled herself together and announced that she was going back inside to look for him and marched off. We met up with her a little while later and she introduced us to Pierre. He was slouching over Emma with his arm around her shoulder and leaning on her as though she was holding him up. He reminded me of an aging rock star, with receding, lanky blonde hair that was too long, wiry thin body and arrogant demeanour. He had no doubt been attractive in his youth and he carried himself as though he still was, but somehow the posturing did not ring true. I could not see the attraction and knowing that Emma's father had left the family at a young age, I was left with the thought that this was Emma's subconscious way of recapturing her childhood. Again, not an unusual tale.

Over the course of our time in Goa, Emma's appearance changed quite dramatically. She lost weight and from being buxom, curvy, and attractive, she became thin, drawn, and tired looking. As she had lost weight so quickly, her skin became loose and one day whilst wearing a low cut top, I noticed that her formally voluptuous bosom had become saggy and wrinkly like the skin of somebody much older. I was aware when I first met her that she was a party animal and also aware that this involved recreational drugs, as she was quite open about this. It seemed, however, that Pierre's influence had turned this from an occasional foray into a daily occurrence. She became jittery when we met up with her now, flitting from one conversational topic to another and not really listening to the responses. She was a little bit jerky and smoked incessantly, so much so that her front teeth became stained with brown nicotine and, whenever she remembered, she took to smiling without opening her mouth properly. She would have made a good before and after model for the marketing campaign "Just say no." It was sad to see.

*

November and December saw us with numerous visitors to the house. Pataj, Nancy's friend from Mumbai, whom I had met when I first arrived at the house, came to stay for a week in November and then for three weeks over Christmas and New Year. He was in Goa to party and organised events to visit nightly. I was always willingly included in these outings, for as long as the company he kept drank and partied alongside him, Pataj was happy. He was a sociable drunk.

He would awake around lunchtime after the night before, put on his music then spend the next hour or so boiling water to pour into buckets to bathe with. Whilst he waited for the pans of water to boil, he would sit outside on the veranda and smoke joints and drink whatever alcohol he had left from the previous night; whisky, rum, or beer. I never saw him sober although I never actually saw him roaring drunk either. He was constantly topped up and obviously his body was very used to vast amounts of alcohol as he never became incoherent or unintelligible. He was pleasant and amiable enough although he treated the house like a hotel, leaving glasses, plates, and bottles wherever he happened to have finished with them, for somebody else to clear away. He was obviously used to servants in his parents' house in Mumbai. As he was always drunk, he was clumsy, constantly knocking things over such as glasses and plates and breaking them. He was a walking danger zone as he would fail to clear up after himself properly and leave broken glass lying around for us to walk upon, treacherous as everybody went barefoot around the house. On one occasion when we had visitors, he accidently tipped a burning candle onto somebody's head setting fire to her hair. Luckily it was noticed and got put out very quickly without too much damage.

Although our house was now twinkling and merry with bunting and fairy lights, the festive feel still eluded us. I had lost my address book since arriving in Goa and although I searched high and low, I never found it. As I had dropped my mobile phone in the sea when I first arrived, I had no contact numbers to ask people back home for their addresses and so; apart from work, my next door neighbour, and my daughter Josie and grandson Otis, no other Christmas cards were sent. Nancy and I had discussed going out for dinner with friends on Christmas day and then spending the afternoon on the beach, however, it did not quite turn out this way. Pataj and Nancy went out to a club on Christmas Eve with a former colleague of Nancy's and her boyfriend who had come down to Goa from Mumbai for the Christmas season. I declined to go out with them, as I wanted to take the computer to a quiet restaurant with an internet connection, so that I could Skype Josie and Otis back in England, to wish them a merry Christmas. They were coming to stay in the New Year and I had bought Josie and her boyfriend Ade Indian presents of scarves and carved jewellery boxes to open when they arrived. Almost every week, I had bought Otis, who was now two, either some Indian clothes or toys, so that he had quite a collection of belated Christmas presents to open on arrival. I was excited.

That evening, after speaking to my family back home, I went home to an empty house and wrapped Christmas presents, still not really feeling the spirit, just missing my family. Nancy and Pataj did not arrive home until lunchtime the following Christmas day. They had danced at the club until sunrise and then went to the beach for a swim; lay on sunbeds until the beach shacks opened, whereupon they ordered and ate breakfast and then slept in the sunshine. I spent Christmas morning alone, worried sick that an accident had befallen Nancy or one of her friends. She walked into the house, laid straight down on her bed, and fell asleep, not even wishing me a "Happy Christmas." Pataj was still partying and poured himself a rum and then went onto the veranda to smoke. He told me the happenings of the previous night.

"Are you still going out for lunch?" I queried, hunger having now displaced the angst.

"Oh, yes," he answered, still full of energy despite his night of dancing.

And so we dined at a little Indian restaurant that was almost empty where I ate chickpea dhal for my Christmas dinner with Pataj and two of Nancy's friends, all of whom were extremely hung over. Conversation was limited and it was a dismal affair. We returned home in the afternoon to find Nancy still flat out, whereupon even

111

Pataj admitted defeat and went to bed. There had been no good wishes, no exchange of presents or cards, no pulling crackers, or games of charades, and certainly no party spirit. In a fit of pique, I tore open the presents of a scarf and blouse that I had bought Nancy and tried them on myself, but I felt no better. I wanted to go back to my home in England and I wanted to go now.

That evening, I rode my scooter to a restaurant in Anjuna that showed current films projected onto a large screen that they hung from the back wall of the restaurant. I was feeling lonely, unhappy, and bored, as both Nancy and Pataj were still fast asleep and I had spent Christmas afternoon sitting on the veranda reading and feeling home sick. The film showing was a horror, which I have always loathed as my vivid imagination comes into play days later, usually late at night when I am home alone. It was just not my Christmas. I ordered an omelette and whilst waiting for my food to arrive, received a text from Nancy asking where I was. I replied to her and she told me to hang on as she would join me. So Nancy and I spent Christmas night together eating omelette and trying to avoid watching and listening to a horror film that was being blasted out of the restaurant speakers. There were only two other people in the venue. I confessed to Nancy that I had opened her presents and was now wearing these. She admired them and laughingly suggested that I keep them, as she had completely forgotten that week that it was Christmas and had not bought anyone any presents. We had a surprisingly nice evening, considering the circumstances, and I followed Nancy home on my scooter feeling quite warm inside, having finally captured a tiny piece of Christmas in my heart.

Chapter 10: Family Matters

My eldest daughter Josie, her partner Ade, and my grandson Otis, who was two years old the previous October, came to stay for two weeks in the New Year. Nancy and I took a taxi to the airport to collect them and we watched them through the plate glass windows of the airport, as they waited for their luggage whilst we waited restlessly outside, the guard refusing us access to the building as we were not flying. Eventually, as the luggage had still not arrived on the carousal, Josie brought Otis to the door of the airport where Nancy and I snatched him from her arms, taking turns to hug and kiss him. He had grown so much in the three months I had been in India and Nancy had not seen him for over six months. He was perfectly happy to come to us despite the fact that he had not seen us in weeks and had been cooped up on a plane for over ten hours. He happily ran around the outside of the airport with us as we waited for Josie and Ade to collect their baggage and come through the doors.

"I spotted you two straight away," Josie said laughing after hugging us, when they eventually collected their luggage and had come through the doors. "Dressed up like Indians the pair of you, I'm surprised you're not wearing saris." The three months in India had changed me I realised. Both Nancy and I were nut brown from riding our bikes in the beautiful Goan sunshine and we both wore the ubiquitous dupatta, Indian style with the ends trailing down our backs, essential for protecting bare arms and shoulders from either mosquitoes or sunshine. We were wearing loose, baggy Indian trousers, that were so cool and comfortable, and an array of bangles and anklets, with Nancy sporting a jewel in the side of her nose and a bindi on her forehead. It was nothing unusual in Goa, but it was certainly a change from my style three months earlier, I realised. We got into the taxi for the journey home and I sat with little Otis upon my knee, holding my hand on the ride back to Anjuna. He was fascinated by the sight of the paper star lanterns that were adorning the shops and restaurants in celebration of Christmas and he happily pointed these out to me all the way back.

The family had booked into a hotel because a package holiday had worked out cheaper than buying just scheduled flights. "Do you want Otis to stay with you tonight?" Josie had asked us, as the taxi drew up to their hotel and she saw the looks on both Nancy's and my face at the thought of letting him go. We were delighted and I had already bought a hammock that I had hung from the rafters and covered in a mosquito net for Otis to sleep in, which we had hung over Nancy's bed in case he tried to climb out. We arrived back at MamaNoo house around midnight and stripped Otis to his vest and nappy before popping him into the hammock and sitting underneath it on Nancy's bed, rocking him to sleep. He was delighted with both the hammock and the rocking motion, and after a few moments of giggling, was fast asleep.

In the morning after breakfast, we took Otis onto the veranda in order to give him a bath. We boiled pans of water and filled one of our large plastic buckets with warm water for him to sit in. He loved it and splashed happily in the water. The Ragamuffin Gang arrived and we introduced them to Otis and they watched as we bathed him, quite fascinated as we towelled him dry and rubbed baby cream into his skin, put a nappy on him, and carefully dressed him in some of the new clothes that I had bought him for Christmas. He was noticeably larger than his Indian counterparts, and though he was not a plump child, he looked positively huge next to baby Yasmi, who never wore nappies or underwear under the invariably filthy dresses that she wore. The children played happily together on the little veranda and were particularly taken with Otis's pushchair that Josie had brought over on the plane with her and which we had brought back to the house with Otis the previous night. We put Yasmi into the push chair, pulling the seat back and raising the front so that she could lay back which she did with obvious delight and the children took it in turns to push her up and down the veranda, some faster and less carefully than others. She was asleep in two minutes. It must have been the first sleep that she had been able to take during the day for a long time and she lay in the pushchair contentedly sleeping whilst the children played.

*

A few nights after they first arrived, Josie and Ade stayed the night with us as at the house. They slept in Nancy's bed with Otis above them in the hammock and complained loudly in the morning about the uncomfortable bed, the cold water, and the scratching noises in the night.

"For goodness sake, Mama, move out and get somewhere decent." Josie had instructed me.

It was not something that I had not even thought about before, but I started to seriously consider the option, having just spent an evening babysitting for Otis whereby the electricity constantly kept tripping out. The main switch would not turn back on for at least ten minutes after it had tripped and so we were continually being plunged into darkness. The toddler was not in the least bit bothered and loved the candle light and torches, but I was terrified that he would knock over a candle and start a fire as there were no shelves on which to place them out of the way. Whilst turning the main switch down on one occasion, I received a nasty electric shock, so much so that I put on two pairs of rubber gloves and flip-flops to switch it back down after that. However, worse than the dark, and chasing Otis around in it as he darted through the curtain doors with ease, was the quiet. As soon as the electricity cut out, the music stopped, and I was terrified of hearing scampering or scratching in the dark. The whole evening was of nightmare proportions.

To add to my already nervous disposition when sleeping in the house, we had come in one night and gone straight to bed, only to be woken by a scratching noise coming from under the foot of my bed. Terrified, I commenced clapping my hands loudly, which was the drill in such circumstances, when suddenly a large pale creature jumped onto the mosquito net at the foot of my bed landing on my legs, before jumping off just as quickly and racing across the room. I screamed loudly, and turned to see a white cat running through the doorway. It must have gained access through the bars of the kitchen window, and been asleep under my bed before we entered the house and disturbed it. None of the windows of the house were glazed and shutters had long ago rotted with the monsoon rains and not been replaced. We were a haven for any visitors who could climb, crawl, walk, or slither into the house. In the same week as the cat incident, Nancy woke me one morning, also screaming. She had been woken up by something falling onto her bed with a heavy thud, presumably from the rafters above, but when she examined the sheet that was covering her, she could not see anything, so she settled back down again. Suddenly, horrors, she felt something heavy crawling onto her head. She let out a piercing scream sitting up shaking her hair with her hands, to see an enormous lizard crawling across her pillow. Enough was more than enough.

During Josie's stay, she and Ade decided to take a trip down to south Goa on a scooter and stay for a few days whilst I, willingly, looked after Otis. We realised that the fully paid up hotel room in which they were staying would be empty and not wanting a repeat of the evening with the power failures, we decided that Otis and I should stay there. We reasoned that the staff would not even notice the change of customer and, besides, it was the same child that I was with, and so that was what we did. The hotel was such bliss and Otis and I spent most of the day in and around the swimming pool and bar area. We ate lunch at the hotel and, if the staff noticed the change of carer for the child, they never mentioned it. We became friendly with a Swedish lady who was also staying at the hotel with her little girl and so we dined with them in the evenings at local restaurants. At night after putting Otis to bed, I laid in the comfortable bed next to him until he was asleep, and then I switched on the television, which was invariably showing a film in English and leaned back on the soft plump pillows. It all felt like such luxury compared to what I was now becoming used to.

After Josie's visit to Goa, life at the house generally became more stressful. Nancy and I seemed to be at loggerheads constantly; she had reverted back to teenage mode, leaving clothes lying about, not helping with the housework and, the worse offence of all, leaving open packets of biscuits and food around which were an open invitation to the furry visitors. To compensate, I had reverted into weary mother mode; I nagged her, cajoled her, told her off, and eventually took on martyr status and just cleared up after her constantly. We both hated it all and the rows became more frequent and furious. I remember thinking after one particularly nasty row that I did not like my daughter very much, I loved her I reasoned, but I did not really like her, and then the eureka moment hit home. This was exactly the same situation as when she was a teenager and then the dynamics had only changed when she left home. We had become the best of friends again after this, right up until now that was. It was definitely time for me to move out.

*

The Saturday Night Market had started on New Year's Eve, just before Josie, Ade and Otis's arrival. We were by then quite experienced as market traders and were pitch perfect with our sales patter. Difficulties arose, however, with the layout of our market stall. Because

118

Nancy was a designer, and our products had not just been bought for resale, we were awarded artisan status that afforded us a prestigious corner stall. We were placed next to one of the drinking bars, an excellent position especially as the stall was open at three sides, allowing it to be viewed from most positions. This meant, however, that the layout of the stall furniture became tricky in terms of where to place it to maximise stock viewing, but to minimise blocking our potential customers from entering the stall. Both Nancy and I had our own ideas about where the furniture should be placed, but Nancy's ideas changed every week. It was another point of argument. In the end, this argument was finalised by Cath who ran a clothes stall across the lane from us. She was an experienced trader who spent half the year in Goa and the other half in Ibiza. She worked the market stalls with her long-term boyfriend and they were a close-knit team. Both Cockneys they were funny, down-to-earth, and generous. They watched us with quiet amusement each week as we arrived to set up our stall and commence our weekly argument about where the furniture should be placed. One Saturday night, after having witnessed this fiasco several times, Cath strolled over to our stall and casually intervened as we were in full debate about where to place the table.

"Hi guys, I 'ope you don't mind me interruptin', but I've been watchin' you every week, an' I reckon I could give you some advice, if you're interested? It's just that you're not maximisin' your sellin' potential. Now, if you were to put some shelves up at the back an' sides, an' get rid of that table, it would open up the stall no end. Make it more invitin'. I think you need to put signs up with your name in huge letters to announce yourselves.

You need to make it easy for the punter to enter, that would make a huge difference to your business. I 'ope you don't mind me telling you?"

We did not mind, as business at Cath's stall was booming, and she was obviously an experienced saleswoman. She was experienced in Goan life too and somebody who might know about potential apartments.

"Cath," I inquired, "You don't happen to know of any apartments for rent do you? Our house has rats and I just can't take it any longer."

"Certainly do, there's an apartment goin' on our complex. How much do you wanna pay?"

I told her my price and she promised to have a chat with her friend who owned the apartment, he was a hardcore walker, apparently, and was presently hiking around India with his girlfriend. Cath was as good as her word and a couple of days later she phoned me to say that she had negotiated my price with the apartment owner and I could come and take a look at it if I was interested. I was!

The apartment was as far removed from our present house as was possible, they were polar opposites. Where MamaNoo House was old and had character, the apartment was new and soulless. Where the house was nestled amongst temples and other houses, the apartment was insular being gated, with patrolling security guards, gardeners, and a caretaker; no free range dogs, cattle, or children wandering around here. It had hot water, air conditioning, sealed walls and ceilings, tiled floors, freshly painted walls, a wardrobe, full size cooker with an oven, and, joy of joys, a swimming pool which was shared between the complex of eight houses and two apartments. Once inside the gates, I could have been anywhere on Earth that had a hot climate; Spain, America, Brazil, anywhere. Never was such a characterless place so welcome. Sorted!

I had to admit to feelings of guilt though in abandoning MamaNoo House, akin to those of leaving a sinking ship. I loved the house, its rural authenticity, the traditional well, the rustic beams, the clay floors that stained our feet an earthy red. I adored being part of a Goan neighbourhood with the regular visits from children, dogs, and cows. The neighbours stopping to chat as they walked past the veranda when we were sat outside, making us feel a part of the fabric of the area. But it was no use, because all of this was overridden by my absolute abhorrence, loathing, and fear of the insects and vermin that also inhabited the house. I had spent too many nights sleeping fitfully, waking up to hear noises, real or imagined, and spending too much of the night clapping my hands to ward off any creatures that I imagined were lurking nearby. I was as characterless as the new apartment, we were a match made in Heaven, so I packed my clothes from MamaNoo House, strapped the case on my scooter, and moved in.

*

Nancy and I took Cath's advice about the market stall and purchased planks of wood, cut to size and drilled, to make shelving and stall signs. We painted the planks black gloss and Nancy painted MamaNoo in gold floaty lettering on three of the pieces. Being a perfectionist, she found a font she liked on her laptop, blew up each letter to maximum size and then traced around these, and then traced this onto each plank. An experienced sign writer could not have produced more perfect signs, they were striking. We set off for the Night Market with our planks balanced precariously on the footwells of our scooters, feet on top. On arrival, we set about making our rope and plank shelving. It was a difficult balancing act to tie heavy plank shelves to our bamboo stall and keep the planks level. There were three planks to both the back and side shelving and we knotted the ropes under each shelf to keep them in place, but the knots slipped and the shelves slanted. It was hard work in the blistering sun and Nancy the perfectionist was becoming frustrated.

"This can't be the proper way to do it. You're just too slap-happy, shoving them up any old way. It looks crap!"

"Nancy, there isn't a science to putting up rope shelving, there's no such thing as perfection. This is a market stall; go and look at everyone else's stalls, they are all haphazard, that's part of the charm."

In the face of not having an answer as to how to tie them up so that they were spirit level straight and stayed that way, Nancy stormed off and left me to it. I struggled alone, but managed to tie them up and kept the shelving straight by an arrangement of stones placed under the knots in the rope, to raise the shelf on the side it was lilting on. It worked, albeit Heath Robinson style, but the shelves were straight enough for products to sit upon and they looked good. Just before I left, I noticed that one shelf was still sloping, so I decided to tighten the rope where it was tied to the bamboo roof. I stood on the old table from the house that we had left at the Night Market to display our goods, when one of its legs broke. I tumbled to the floor. I must have let out a cry because several of the cleaning women who were working around the market ran towards me to assist. They were very kind and helped me to my feet and dusted me down. They led me to the steps nearby to sit down and brought me a drink of water. I was shaken and bruised, but no real harm done. Ah well, that was the end of the table, one of the few items of furniture that the house possessed.

Nancy was contemplating staying in the house by herself after I moved out, but after a couple of weeks she announced that she too was leaving as she wanted to be nearer to the centre of Anjuna. She had found a house that was quite near to the town centre and the beach; it was in an area where the original hippies had settled when they first arrived in Goa in the 60's. It was just next door to the German Bakery, which was a popular dining venue that also had live entertainment. As I had only taken my clothes from MamaNoo House and left the rest of the belongings we had accumulated, she asked me if I would help her to pack, and to tidy and clean the house. Nancy had arranged for a large taxi to come and take the furniture and household wares to her new abode.

The Ragamuffin Gang soon spotted us and came around to watch what we were doing. We explained that we were packing our belongings as we were leaving the house. There were tears and protestations. Nancy drove her scooter to the little cabin at the top of the road and brought back piles of sweets and chocolates and we sat on the veranda and divided the spoils between the children. Nancy whispered to me that she was going to give Laysa some money; she looked after all of the children and we were both very fond of her, she was such a lovely young girl, with such a tough life. Unlike the other children, Laysa never asked for anything from us, although she would gratefully accept any food or drink that was offered. Quite often the children would ask us for money, although we never gave them any, as we knew that demands would be constant if we did. It is common for poor Indian people to beg off western tourists, as we are perceived as affluent in their eyes, which indeed we are in comparison. Nancy sidled up to Laysa and slipped a 100 rupee note into her hand, the equivalent of about 80 pence in sterling; not a great deal, but a lot to a poor child in India. Laysa opened her hand and looked at the money and then came over to Nancy and gave the money straight back, shaking her head, and looking cross. Nancy tried to give it to her again, but she refused adamantly. We were puzzled by her behaviour and Nancy suggested that perhaps she had been told never to take money off strangers, but then we remembered that when we had first met her older sister, she had immediately asked us for money much to Laysa's obvious embarrassment and anger. For some reason, Laysa had risen above the poverty of her upbringing and had a quiet dignity and pride about her. Her message to us was loud and clear; she was our friend and not a beggar child. And so we all sat down on the veranda, and Laysa, as usual, fed baby Yasmi the sweets first before she ate anything herself. Then with mouths full of sweets; the boys stuffing handfuls in at once, all cheekily competing with one another, we sang "Yellow Submarine" at the top of our voices, with no care if the neighbours liked it or not. It was another of the children's favourite songs and, again, one in which the only part we could remember was the chorus. Then, after hugs and tears, we rode away from the little red house for the last time, whilst the children stood in line waving at us, with baby Yasmi perched on Laysa's hip, just like always.

Chapter 11: Burma

One of the first people we met when arriving in Arpora was Burma. She was a neighbour of ours at MamaNoo House and rented a room nearby where she lived with her mother-in-law, her husband, some of their children, and their grandchildren. About eight people in total. They were migrant workers from Karnataka who were here for the season to make some money before returning home to work as farm labourers. Burma was a constant throughout our time in Goa, one of the first people we met when we arrived and one of the last we visited to say goodbye.

Burma was a small, plump woman about mid 40's to 50 in age. She always wore bright coloured, gilded saris, and short tops so that rolls of midriff were constantly on display. She was often smiling and had the advantage over other migrant workers from Karnatika in that she could speak a smattering of English, and what she lacked in vocabulary she certainly made up for in confidence. Burma was not a shy person. Whenever I saw her she gave the impression that she was about to go out somewhere special, as she would be wearing gold earrings, plenty of gold bangles and anklets and gold chains about her neck. Her eyes were always heavily made-up with kohl and she would sport a large red bindhi on her forehead and quite often one in her hairline too. She was glamorous in her own inimitable way.

When Kate, Nancy, and I arrived at the house from the airport on the first day in Goa and were carrying in our cases from the taxi, Burma came along the path, smiling at us. She confidently walked into our front garden, went through the veranda gates, and sat down on one of the benches, quite at home. She spoke to Santosh, the landlord, in Hindi and he translated that she was asking if we liked the house. Apparently, Santosh had hired her to clean the house and tidy up the garden prior to our arrival, as it had been left unoccupied for a while. We told her that we liked it; according to Nancy who had viewed it prior to the clean up, she had done a good job. Speaking through Santosh she asked us if we needed her to clean for us, but we told her that with three women in the house, we would be able to clean it ourselves, but thanked her for the offer. Santosh advised us that if we did decide to have a cleaner, then Burma was the woman to have, as she could be trusted. She then offered to do massages for us and as a demonstration of her prowess, went over to Kate and started to kneed her shoulders. Kate looked at me and shuddered whispering, "I hate being massaged." Again we declined her offer saying that we were tired and were going inside now to rest. She smiled at us unperturbed. Santosh left us, and we went inside the house for tea and biscuits before bed, but still Burma sat quite contently on our veranda. Kate and I went to bed and Nancy told us that it was a good 20 minutes later before Burma stood up and waddled down the road back to her room.

Every day after that Burma would call at the house and in her broken English and with sign language offer to clean and do massages for us. We always politely declined. She never took offence and would plonk herself down on the veranda seats smiling at us, often staying for a while whether invited to or not. She sometimes called round with her grandchildren, either two little boys or a little girl, but never brought all three children together. The two little boys were brothers and polar opposites in personalities. The youngest, around two years old, was incredibly shy, hiding behind his older brother, whenever he was spoken to. The eldest boy, who was about four, had not only inherited Burma's physique being small and stocky, but also her personality. He was confident and boisterous, running around the veranda and jumping off the wall, constantly grinning at us and checking that we were watching him. He would sing Bollywood songs for us and dance in the style of the male heroes, jumping off the veranda wall and landing on his feet then flinging his arms open wide as he knelt down on one knee in a grand finale. He had it off pat and was quite hilarious. Unlike many of the other migrant workers' children, Burma's grandchildren were supervised during the day whilst their parents and grandparents worked. We often saw their elderly great-grandmother sitting on a plastic chair outside of their room, whilst the children played on the little path in front of the building. They were bigger than most of the other local children too, not overweight, but not with stick thin arms and legs either. They were obviously well cared for and wore clean clothes without tears and sported clean faces, unlike the poor Ragamuffin Gang children.

One day Kate was sat on the veranda having a cigarette whilst I was in the shower and Burma called round. As they were chatting Burma was trying to persuade Kate that what she needed was a massage to relieve her stress. Kate was equally insistent that she did not have any stress to relieve. In an effort to further befriend her and engage Kate in her services, Burma suggested that Kate come with her to visit her home. Kate politely declined, but as Burma insisted she began to feel rude and so agreed to go with her. They walked up the dirt track to the top of the road where Burma rented a room within a house, it had its own entrance down a side road. Kate said that the room was dark, about 20 square feet in diameter and piled with bedding and clothing around the walls of the room. There was no furniture save for one plastic chair in which Burma's mother-in-law was sitting. She got up and greeted Kate warmly. Burma insisted that they all have chai, so Kate sat on a mat on the floor whilst Burma put the kettle on. The stove consisted of an open fire on the floor of the room near to the small open window frame where the fumes could escape. The room was home to Burma and around eight of her relatives; it must have been a tight squeeze when all of the bed rolls were laid out at night. As Burma was the only person in the family who spoke any English and little at that, conversation was stilted. Kate drank her chai, thanked Burma warmly for her hospitality, and left to walk back up the dirt road to MamaNoo House.

Burma called round to the house a few days later with her two grandsons who were both wearing dinosaur hats. Through sign language and broken English ascertained that Burma had made these for the children out of scraps of material. They consisted of a hood that fastened under the chin, with two felt ears on top and a long tail which went down the children's back with triangles of felt type cloth sewn all the way down the middle, like spiny protuberances. The children looked so cute and were obviously thrilled with them; even the youngest managed a shy grin. Burma explained that they needed hats as the weather was so cold now because it was winter. As far as we were concerned it was roasting hot and even a sheet at night became too warm. However, covering babies and children's heads during the winter months seemed to be a theme in Goa and we would often see the smallest of babies and toddlers sporting the most enormous woolly hats despite the blazing sunshine.

*

When Nancy and I started the markets we realised that we had no way of transporting the chair to the markets each week and it had taken so much effort to send it from Mumbai to Goa. It was too big to put on the back of a scooter and there was no storage at the markets. We could have chained and padlocked the chair to the stall, but with such a valuable item, somebody was sure to cut the chain or simply pull out the bamboo corner post, which was all we could chain it to. Then one day when Burma came to visit, Nancy suggested to her that she carry the chair to the Night Market each week and bring it back for us; about a 15 to 20 minute walk. We arranged a fee and every day that week prior to the Saturday, Burma arrived at the house anxiously checking the arrangements again. At the allotted time on the Saturday, Burma appeared and the chair was carried off to the market on her head. During the first market, Burma came to our stall and introduced us to her husband who would be collecting the chair to take home again when the market was beginning to go quiet, around two in the morning. Burma herself had secured the task of cleaning some of the market toilets and so she would be finished later than this. She asked us if she could keep the chair at her house, but as we had so little furniture in our own house, we needed this to sit on. So it was arranged that they would take it home and then return it to us the following morning each week, everybody pleased with these arrangements.

Burma's husband carried an air of long suffering about him. He was a tall, spindly man who always wore white Indian style dress and a paper hat, the type seen in Britain on the servers in fast food restaurants. He had a kind of humble demeanour, always very reverent, greeting and leaving us with "Namaste" and bowing low with his hands together in prayer. At first we used to worry about him carrying the chair as he seemed rather frail, staggering as he picked it up to put it onto his head. However, we soon came to realise that this was actually because he was so often drunk and nothing at all to do with his physique. We would drive past him in the early hours of the morning as we left the Night Market, our scooters loaded up with the contents of the stall, and there he would be staggering down the road with our chair plonked lopsidedly on his head. One night we drove past him and he had put the chair down on the side of the road and was sitting on it, laid back peacefully staring at the stars whilst enjoying a cigarette.

Burma and her husband also worked at the Wednesday Flea Market as coolies, carrying the stallholders' goods from scooters and vans to the stalls for a small fee. As the stalls were built on dirt that was dry and dusty from the sun, the coolies would also go around the stalls with pots of water and sprinkle this onto

131

the ground in front of a stall to stop the dust flying up and covering the stock, again for a small fee, of course. Burma had a trick of sprinkling the water before the stallholder had arrived or when they had gone off somewhere, and then she would return later to demand her ten rupees fee, becoming quite agitated when the stallholder refused to pay. She tried it with us a few times until we got wise to her and sprinkled our own water on the ground first, before she got around to us. The money was not much, but the scams were constant and so we had to draw the line somewhere, being on a tight budget. Whilst on sprinkling duty, Burma would tuck her sari up around her knees to stop it becoming wet and pour the water between her legs whilst walking backwards. It was a comical sight to watch, as for all her weight she had very skinny, bowed legs which were totally out of proportion to the rest of her body, which looked even larger with masses of sari material gathered around her waist.

*

The last month that Nancy and I were in the house together, we decided that rather than keep arguing over whose turn it was to do the housework, it would be easier to ask Burma to do it on a weekly basis after all. The next time we saw Burma we put the proposition to her and she was absolutely delighted. She arrived the next day and tucking up her sari as she did at the market, she set to with gusto. Nancy and I went out for a couple of hours whilst she was still hard at it, scrubbing, dusting, and polishing. Such was her enthusiasm for the task that she stood on a plastic chair and, with a long pole in her hands, dusted the open beams of the ceiling in every room; thick dust and cobwebs came tumbling down. Her short little vest rode up as she stretched to reach the cobwebs, so much so, that at one point a large pendulous breast fell out and flopped onto her abdomen. She was not in the least bit perturbed, however, merely cackling out loud whilst vigorously tucking it back in. When we returned later she was just finishing the job, it had taken her almost four hours. She was sweaty and dirty and looked tired, but elated. She smiled at us both as we entered the dining room and then plonking herself down onto a chair, she leaned back, stuck her legs out in front of her and in a loud voice demanded, "Chai!"

Every week it became a ritual that Burma would clean for us and then when she had finished the task, she announced this by plonking herself down on a chair and demanding that we make her chai. Before she left each week she would point to some item in the house such as a towel, a chair, cutlery, or crockery and ask if we would give it to her. As we did not have anything to spare, we always declined her request, but she did not seem to mind or take offence at our refusal, merrily asking again the next time she came. Whether she intended using these items or selling them was unclear, but what was clearly apparent was that Burma was constantly on the make.

Nancy stayed at the MamaNoo House on her own for a couple of weeks after I had moved out, before moving out herself. I returned to the house to help her pack and clean up. As usual, Burma came waddling along the road to see what was happening. We explained that we were moving out. At first she did not comprehend and then when she had ascertained that her suspicions were correct, she burst into tears, hugging us both and wailing,

"My friends, my friends." It was quite a performance. Then, sensibility kicked in and she realised that we may be leaving things behind. She started to help us move stuff out of the house onto the veranda and every single item that she moved she asked could she have. She eventually waddled up the road loaded with a hairbrush, some of Nancy's t-shirts, and armfuls of paper decorations and lanterns that we had hung around the veranda and which neither of us wanted to transport to our new abodes. I do not know what Burma intended doing with these, but she was obviously delighted with her spoils. I pictured her dark little room being festooned with lanterns and streams of bright paper flowers. It was a nice thought.

Chapter 12: Rancheta

Rancheta was also an Indian neighbour at MamaNoo House. She was a beautiful young woman, 27 years old, who dressed in traditional Indian attire with her hair in a bun at the nape of her neck. We had been at the house for around a week when she called to introduce herself. She spoke broken English and told us that she was married and rented a room in the house at the side of ours with her young husband. She proudly told us that it was a love marriage and not arranged. She used to work as a fruit seller, hawking her produce on her head, up and down the beach of Candolim where she was born and where her widowed mother still lived; it was about eight miles away from Arpora where we lived. However, since her marriage two years ago, her husband did not like her working on the beach and so she now worked as a housekeeper, cleaning and cooking for an Indian family who lived locally. She only worked part-time and we got the impression that she was rather bored as she often came over to our house to pass time with us. She was a font of information and taught us so much about Indian culture and customs.

Her husband worked from home having undertaken an electronics course and now repaired mobile phones and computers. He was also very attractive, with a macho swagger about him, racing up and down the dirt lane to the houses on a large motorbike, quite a status symbol in the area, as most people drove the cheaper scooters. Nancy had an iTouch with all her music on it, but the screen had suddenly gone blank and would not come back on; she asked Rancheta if her husband could fix it. Rancheta said she would take it to him to look at. She returned that evening to say that he had looked at it and thought he could fix it, but that it would need a new screen and it would cost around 5,000 rupees, about 35 pounds sterling at that time. Nancy said that this was too expensive and that she would pay up to 1,000 rupees, but no more. Rancheta informed us that her husband would look at it and see what he could do. She returned the next day with a repaired iTouch, stating that this would cost 1,000 rupees. Nancy happily paid the bill, thrilled that she could play music again and look at her photographs; apparently it had not needed a new screen.

Whenever the home-owner's children were off school for the summer holidays, Rancheta would hang around with a couple of the teenage girls, one of whom was the sister of Rakmir, our young taxi driver. Rancheta came around to the house one day with her two young friends in tow, both of whom spoke very good English, they were both 14. It was after Kate had left Goa and just Nancy and I were at home. Nancy had been practicing hula hooping on the veranda when Rancheta and her friends called to visit. Nancy had been into hooping for several years and was very proficient in it, doing amazing tricks and feats with the hoop; swinging it around her neck, legs, and arms. Obviously, this took lots of practice, like most hobbies, and Nancy had brought a selection of hoops with her to the house. We chatted to Rancheta and friends and asked what was at the back of our house, as we often saw the workers walking past our house into the fields at the back. They explained that this was a shortcut across the fields into Anjuna town and that it consisted of a river and lots of scrubland, where the children played cricket. They offered to take us there to look.

We all traipsed off to explore and Nancy, as an afterthought, grabbed a hula hoop to take with her, and so copying her, the girls picked up the rest of the hoops. In the beautiful Indian sunshine we had an afternoon of fun and innocence in the fields behind the MamaNoo house. We all took it in turns to hoop and Rancheta and the girls taught us Bollywood dancing, Rancheta being something of an expert in the genre. We got the impression that these films were followed very closely with every move analysed. We went down to the river-bank which was surrounded by bulrushes and the girls showed us some strange creatures that lived in the mud of the sloping bank. If we waited, very still, what looked like hundreds of single crab pincers would emerge from the silt, and wave in the air. At the slightest movement, the vibrations would cause the creatures to bury back down. We watched for ages, as the sight of thousands of small, pale pink pincers waving in the air was mesmerising. We would stay very still and then quickly move, watching the creatures swaying in the air and then hurriedly burying back into the mud. A few crawled out of the silt completely and they were tiny creatures like large grains of rice waving a single comparatively huge pincer above them, it being about four times the size of their trunks; they did not have heads, legs, or other appendages, just the single pincer; a very weird creature indeed.

On the way back home, the girls also showed us a tree that had a delicious fruit they informed us. We had often seen members of the Ragamuffin Gang eating this fruit and had wondered what it was. It looked like an olive, in that it was the same size and shape and contained a similar stone, but it had skin like an apple that was coloured a mixture of green and red. The girls hit the branches with sticks to make the fruit fall down onto the ground. They then examined each fallen fruit carefully and picked some out and threw others away. We could not tell what the criteria was for selecting the fruit, as they all looked the same to us, but the girls cautioned us not to eat certain ones, so we obeyed. On tasting the delicious fruit, we discovered that they were dry and bitter, an obvious cultural taste difference that we did not manage to bridge — horrible!

*

To supplement our income at the Saturday Night Market, in addition to selling our stock, we offered face painting. It was very popular as the market had a party atmosphere as, in addition to the hundreds of stalls, it also had live music, bars, and fast-food stalls. At first, just Nancy did the face painting, but as it was so popular and often quite busy, I also started to paint and, much to Nancy's chagrin, I became quite well liked, with several customers specifically requesting my skills. We had quite a different style of face painting, Nancy preferring bold, clear strokes, whilst I favoured finer more intricate designs with lots of glitter and bling in the form of stick-on plastic jewels. I particularly liked painting the Aztec designs in gold, bronzes, black, and metallic reds, which the men tended to like. It was good fun and we always painted our own faces as soon as we arrived at the market, as a walking advertisement for our product and our styles.

One day whilst at home, we decided that we needed a booklet of photographs depicting the different face painting styles that we offered, so customers could choose the specific style they liked. We already had a couple of photographs to show people, but this was rather limited and we had now branched into various other styles such as flowers and harlequins. Rancheta was at our house at the time we were discussing this and so we asked her if she would model for us, she delightedly agreed. Nancy painted her face with a swirling design and added glitter and plastic jewels, finishing with a jewelled bindi placed in the centre of the red bindi that she already wore indicating that she was a married woman. She was absolutely thrilled with the effect, studying her face in the mirror from all angles. She then rushed home to show her husband, before returning to start over again with another design. She was very photogenic and we captured some excellent photographs of our designs painted on Rancheta's beautiful visage.

*

Later on in our relationship with Rancheta, we discovered to our surprise that she lived up to her name. I had brought an iPhone with me from England and when I eventually secured an Indian SIM card, the phone still would not work, as it was locked to the original service provider. In despair, I bought a cheap Indian phone to use instead. However, I was unable to get onto the internet with this new phone, nor could I use the free phone call and text message applications that were available on my other phone. I was missing Josie, my daughter in England, and my gorgeous grandson Otis, and it was too expensive to call them on a regular basis from my Indian phone. When chatting to an English friend one day, he informed me that the original phone providers usually offered a service, whereby, for a fee, they can email details of how to unlock phones, thus enabling other SIM cards to work. I phoned the company, paid by credit card, and they emailed me the code to unlock my phone. Hallelujah! I had a glorious day of Skyping, calling, texting, and forwarding photographs to my daughter and my friends in England for free. However, my bliss was short-lived.

At the time of being reunited with my phone, Nancy's Indian friend, Pataj, had just arrived at the house and we all arranged to go to a party that evening at one of the beach bars in Anjuna. It was a good night out and we dined at the bar and then partook of plenty of drinks throughout the evening. At around two o'clock in the morning, full of merriment, we happily walked along the beach to the centre of Anjuna, hoping to find a taxi to take us home. At one point in the walk, when we were scrambling over rocks in the dark, I sat down on a rock to swing my legs over to the other side, rather than climb over it. Unbeknown to me, my cloth shoulder bag had swung into a rock pool and the contents of the bag, including my phone, were dangling in the water.

"Don't worry, Mama," Nancy assured me when I realised what had happened, "I dropped mine down the toilet once, but I put it in rice and it worked fine afterwards. We'll just open it up and put it in a bowl of dried rice when we get home."

140

We did just that, and in the morning I put the phone back together, but still no joy, the screen was completely dead. Wondering if the battery needed charging, I plugged it into a socket, whereby I noticed a strange electrical burning smell and nothing else. The phone had been murdered by drowning and electrocution and, to make matters worse, I had been the unwitting executioner. I was devastated. For one brief day I had experienced the joys of free texting and phoning, and now it had been taken away from me again. Rancheta called round and I told her the sad tale of my phone, she, inappropriately, roared laughing and kept imitating me plugging in the phone, shaking her head and saying, "No, no no, Nancy's mother, no, no, no!" I asked if her husband would take a look at it and, laughingly, she agreed to take it to him, still shaking her head in wonder at my stupidity as she went.

She called back later that day to say that her husband could fix the phone, but that he would have to order parts from the city to replace what had been burned out when I plugged it into the socket. This was the worst thing I could have done, she told me cheerfully. She asked me for 5,000 rupees to purchase the parts. I agreed and handed over the money. I did not see Rancheta for about a week after this, which was unusual. I saw her coming out of her house one day and asked her about my phone, she said that it was worse than originally thought and her husband needed further parts before it could be fixed. It would cost another 5,000 rupees to buy these parts. I reasoned that this was still much cheaper than buying a similar phone and so handed over the money and, again, I did not see Rancheta or her husband for around a week. By now, I was beginning to get a little anxious about this behaviour, as Rancheta was usually a regular visitor. Nancy was quite enraged about the whole episode and called round to Rancheta's house on my behalf, to demand either the repaired phone or my money back. Rancheta was home alone and informed her that she would call tomorrow with the repaired phone, explaining that it was delayed because her husband had been waiting for a part to arrive. Tomorrow never came, nor the next tomorrow, nor the next. Eventually, around a month after the day I first gave the phone to Rancheta, she called at the house with a similar phone to mine, saying that her husband could not repair the original phone as it was too badly damaged, but that he had bought this phone for me instead. I was quite happy with the arrangement, for despite it being an older version of my phone, it seemed a fair deal, although I was a little bemused by all the tales of repairs that had been recounted to us previously. On trying to connect to the internet that evening, however, I discovered that the phone would not work properly. A friend took a look at it and informed me that it was a fake iPhone that could be used for calls and texts only, in short, it was no better than the cheap Indian phone that I had already purchased.

Again, Rancheta and her husband were nowhere to be seen for several days. I did eventually see her husband leaving the house one day and so took the opportunity to confront him. I gave him back the fake phone and demanded my original phone back and the money I had paid to him. He went inside and returned with my phone, still broken of course, stating that he would pay back the 5,000 rupees owing when he was paid at the end of that week. I told him it was 10,000 rupees that he owed me, and he looked genuinely shocked. Obviously, Rancheta had been deceiving both of us. I was disappointed, shocked, and hurt by her behaviour, because I had really liked her and thought of her as a friend. They eventually paid back half of the money owing, in drip form, a little each week.

Nancy and I often pondered over Rancheta's strange behaviour, did she really think that I would ignore the fact that she had taken my hard earned money? Did we seem stupid to her? They must have known from the start that the phone was beyond repair and surely they must have realised I would not be happy with a fake phone. On reflection, we realised that it must have appeared like we had an endless stream of money; I could spend a week's worth of her wages on getting a phone repaired, when I already had one that worked perfectly. We lived in a large house full of electronic gadgets including computers, whereas she and her husband rented a small room. We only worked a couple of days a week and yet we were still affluent. We reasoned that the temptation to take my money must have been overwhelming and she, no doubt, reasoned that I would not really miss it and hoped that I would not ask for it back. It was a risky game she played though, because if we had called the police to investigate, they both could have got into a lot of trouble. The Goan authorities are keen to cut down on tourist crime so as not to discourage visits to the area, this being the mainstay of income for this region. When I came to leave the MamaNoo house the following week I was still owed 5,000 rupees and, despite Rancheta promising that she would bring the money to the market the following Saturday, I never saw her again, of course. As her name implied, she was a cheater who ran!

Chapter 13: A Lonesome State of Mind

I settled into my new apartment very quickly, but after the initial euphoria of moving house had dissipated I became quite lonely. The apartment was at the bottom of some small mountains and the phone signal was none existent, meaning that I could not access either the internet or my phone. Nancy's house was positioned under a canopy of trees in a wooded area, so her phone connection was also dubious. I was effectively cut off from contacting my only social partner. I had by now become far more confident on the scooter and would hop on it and drive around with a fairly good geographical knowledge of the immediate area. When I was not at the markets working, I would go out for lunch and dinner, go shopping at the local supermarkets, go to the beach, go to yoga sessions, drive to Nancy's house, or go to internet cafes to write emails and my blog, but I did not have any friends whom I could call on and I was feeling the strain of my own company. I decided that this had to change. If I wanted to meet people, then it was up to me to start talking to folk and soon.

On my iPod that I had brought with me from home, I had a recording of a motivational speaker who was addressing issues of self-confidence. I had downloaded it along with several other recordings but had not listened to it previously. Now was the time, I thought, to start listening as it might help me to find the confidence I needed to make new friends. I am quite a reserved person until I am familiar with people and find it difficult to start conversations with strangers, not being naturally chatty. The speaker suggested that affirmations were a helpful way in which to overcome issues of shyness and lack of confidence and that these affirmations should be repeated constantly. I came up with the affirmation "I am calm, confident, and charismatic, people are very attracted to me." I repeated it constantly to myself, whenever I was going anywhere on my bike I would say it over and over again in my head. I told Nancy about my affirmation and she adopted it too, and we would yell it out to each other laughing.

Emma, a friend of ours, had mentioned a therapist that she was seeing about her hips and legs. When Emma had first arrived in Goa in October, she had come off her scooter when going over a road bump at speed and had fractured her skull and pelvis. She was hospitalised for around a week and then sent home. Although she soon recovered, she was suffering from aches and pains in her pelvis and legs and was meeting with a therapist who specialised in cranial-sacral therapy, which gently assists in putting the body back into alignment. She recommended it as I was suffering with a sore back, due, I thought, to the awful bed that I had been sleeping on at the MamaNoo house. Even though the bed at the apartment was quite comfortable, my back was still sore and causing me problems with constant aching. I took the name and phone number of the therapist off Emma and made an appointment.

Veronica, the therapist, was Canadian, she was lovely; friendly and professional. The therapy session lasted an hour and I felt so much better afterwards, my back was much looser as though tight muscles had relaxed. I was arranging a follow-up session with her for the next week, when she also recommended yoga for my back, telling me that she took yoga classes too and that the first session was free to newcomers. I arranged to go to her class the following morning. As it turned out I was the only participant, but was assured that this was not a problem as it allowed Veronica to practice her yoga and she really did not mind a one-to-one session. A private lesson for free, how amazing. She was a patient, experienced teacher and the lesson lasted 90 minutes. I was floating on air at the end of it, fully in the zone. It became the first of many one-to-one sessions.

After I left the class, still floating high in the clouds, I called at the supermarket near to where I lived to buy some food for lunch. As I walked into the shop I noticed a tall man stood in the doorway; still in the yoga zone I gave him a beatific smile and walked on. I was lost in choosing groceries when I heard somebody talking, I looked up. The man had followed me into the shop and was saying something to me in a foreign language. I looked behind to make sure that it was me he was addressing, there was nobody else around.

"I'm sorry, but I don't understand," I told him.

He repeated himself in what sounded like French.

"I'm sorry." I said, "I only speak English."

"You har not French?" he looked aghast. "I ham so sorry, I thought you were French, you har so helegarnt; you look so French!"

He spoke loudly and his accent was so rich he sounded like a caricature of a French man speaking English, reminiscent of Inspector Clouseau. Still in the

146

zone, I smiled at him. He introduced himself holding out his hand.

"Please excuse me, my name is Jean-Philippe and I ham an harteest"

I shook his hand telling him my name and asking him what sort of art he specialised in.

"Please, allow me to show you," he insisted. "I 'aff some prints in my scooter outside."

He ran off and returned with a small portfolio which held prints of his artworks. He painted the most beautiful pictures of Indian deity taken, he informed me, from sketches he drew of sculptures found in temples.

"Jeeel, I am 'avin an hexhibeeetion on Friday at the gallereee where I show my work. I would be 'onoured 'eef you would come along, my dear."

He gave me his card and then flung his Indian scarf over his shoulder and dramatically flounced out of the shop. I was left feeling bemused. Was he chatting me up or was he drumming up business? Did he fancy me or was he gay? He was tall, slim, and bronzed with a receding hairline and clear, hazel-green eyes, and, obviously, a rather dramatic personality. Overall, he was quite attractive. He was about my age I guessed. He had been wearing long shorts and a vest with the Om peace sign printed on the front and an Indian patterned scarf about his neck. I looked at the card, the exhibition was shared with some other artisans, one of whom was a business rival of ours from the markets who were showcasing their new stock of handbags — we would have to go! I called at Nancy's house to tell her and we arranged to meet up on the Friday evening to travel together.

147

On Friday evening Nancy and I arrived at the venue, which was a beautiful large Goan house on the outskirts of a neighbouring town about a half hour's ride from Anjuna. The house also doubled up as a showroom for the owners' jewellery stock, which was made on the premises in the workrooms located at the back of the house. The owners also sold stock for other artisans and artists and Jean-Philippe sold his paintings here. A huge painting of Ganesh, the Indian elephant deity, was hanging outside of the porch to the house as we walked in and I recognised it as Jean-Philippe's work.

"That's one of his, Nancy." I pointed out.

"Ooh nice," she answered. "I love Ganesh."

We walked into the porch and debated whether to take our shoes off or not. It is custom in India to remove one's shoes when entering a house, but this was also a shop. We erred on the side of caution and removed our shoes and opened the door. The house was elegant and grand with plaster walls painted in pastel shades, tall ceilings, and a sweeping staircase. Elegant, arty looking people were floating about with glasses of wine and little plates of nibbles, everybody was wearing their shoes we noticed self-consciously. We walked around the rooms looking at the jewellery, clothes, and handbags that were displayed and at Jean-Philippe's artworks that were hung in every room. We entered a large room at the front of the house which was lined with jewellery cases, Jean-Philippe was in the corner talking to a lady and he waved at me in a dramatic fashion and soon came over. He kissed me fondly on both cheeks and I introduced him to Nancy.

"Thees is your daughter, I do not believe it, my dear, you look so young!!"

I could sense Nancy inwardly cringing as she hated it when people said this, never knowing if they meant that I looked young or she looked old, and we seemed to be hearing it such a lot since we arrived in Goa due to us being together so much.

"Let me show you both around and explain my hart." Jean-Philippe offered.

He took us on a guided tour of the house, explaining the intricacies of his artwork in great detail. He was flamboyant and waved his arms around expressively as he spoke, reminding me of John Gielgud in some dramatic moment. At the end of it he smiled.

"I aff a leetle more business 'ere and then I am going out for something to eat, would you like to join me?" he asked.

Nancy explained that she was meeting a friend who was flying in from Mumbai and so had to leave shortly for the airport, however, I was free and here was my chance to make new friends.

"I would love to join you." I said.

Jean-Philippe beamed at me delighted.

"I will come and get you in ten minutes," he announced.

Nancy and I looked around at the jewellery on display. They were mostly high-end pieces of traditional European design, which although very beautiful were not to either of our tastes.

"Mama, come and look at this." Nancy said.

One cabinet was filled with the most unusual, ethnic jewellery made from precious metal and stones. It was breathtaking and quite magnificent.

"Oh wow!" I said in amazement.

A smallish man of about Nancy's age came over to us. He had blonde dreadlocks tied back into a ponytail and friendly eyes.

"Hi, I'm Daniel, this is my jewellery."

We told him how much we liked his work and he began to explain a little about the pieces. Nancy had fallen in love with a pendant of silver and copper design that was fashioned using the Japanese art of Mokume-gane, in which different metals are layered on top of each other causing beautiful patterns to arise. The metal had shaped itself into a map of India and a small ruby had been placed in the spot where Goa was. It was very unusual. I was quite taken with a pendant of a serene female face fashioned from what looked to be creamy brown horn. Daniel explained that it represented Tara the Tibetan goddess of compassion and that it was carved from a mammoth tusk.

"But aren't mammoths extinct?" I asked confused.

He explained that with the icecaps shrinking, thousands of mammoth skeletons were becoming exposed, including the tusks that were a source of natural ivory.

Nancy had turned 30 the first weekend that she had come to live at the house in Goa and although we had celebrated at the time, I had only bought her a few cheap presents as she had wanted a silver bangle and we had not seen any that she had liked. I now suggested that instead of a bangle I bought her the pendant. She was thrilled. I reasoned that I also needed to buy myself a memento to commemorate my time in India; I was not going to let Tara go now that I had seen her. I put down a deposit on both pieces.

Nestled Amongst Temples

Nancy went to collect her friend from the airport and Jean-Philippe and I went for dinner. He was good company; funny, relaxed, and quite spiritual. He had spent the last six years visiting India to sketch the statues of deity and then reproduce these in acrylic on canvas in his studio in Paris. He spent around four months of the year in India. He loved the country, the people and the spirituality of India he told me. He walked me to my scooter and then, unexpectedly put his arms around me and kissed me passionately. So that ended that mystery, he was certainly not gay. He then very dramatically flung his lungi, a large Indian scarf, over his shoulder, climbed aboard his scooter, and zoomed off into the night having taken my phone number in order to arrange another meet-up. Well, that was one friend secured and I had only just started looking. The power of the mind eh!

*

One day when Nancy and I were living together we had gone out on our scooters and had stopped to buy fresh coconut milk from a street seller at the side of the road. A man who was obviously hiking, as he was wearing boots and carried a walking pole, also stopped for a drink and we got talking. He told us his name was Steve and he was from Manchester — neighbours! He lived in Goa for the season and was a professional gambler, so he could travel anywhere in the world that had good internet connections. He was another hardcore walker and had hiked the Santiago Trail the previous year and dedicated the experience to his mum. He told us about a place to meet in Arpora for Sunday brunch that was run by a German couple and did a wonderful buffet at a reasonable price. We parted ways promising to meet up for brunch that Sunday. Sure enough we met up and were introduced to Emma who became firm friends with both Nancy and myself (the same Emma that introduced me to Veronica). Emma and Steve had met the last two seasons in which they were both in Anjuna. This was a place where people returned season after season I was beginning to discover.

Steve and I often found ourselves orientating towards each other when out socialising as we both belonged to the same social group that consisted of younger people. As is common when living abroad, we tended to hang around with other Brits and so continually found ourselves in each other's company. He was easy going, friendly, and good fun. I was always more willing to attend a rave or trance party if I knew that he would be there, as it meant that I would have somebody to chat to whilst Nancy and friends danced to the interminable music. He organised a small walk one day along the beach in Morjim that turned out to be just him, Emma, and myself. It was at a relaxing pace as Emma still had trouble walking fast and far since her scooter accident, but the company was good and we had plenty of laughs along the way. Now, Steve would have been a perfect ally to have when I lived on my own, but at this point he had taken off to South Goa to spend some time there.

The day following my dinner with Jean-Phillipe, I received a text from Steve telling me that he was back in Anjuna and asking me if I wanted to undertake a four day hike with him from North to South Goa the following week. I texted back that I would love to and we arranged to meet at the end of the week to take a training hike in preparation. I had only just put down the phone from texting Steve when another text came through, this time from John, whom I had been introduced to one evening when a crowd of us went out for dinner several weeks previously. We had swapped phone numbers at the time and then I had forgotten all about it. He had texted to invite me to join him for dinner one evening that week. This was incredible. In the space of a few days I was inundated with people inviting me out, so much for my loneliness.

Chapter 14: North to South Goa

I had readily accepted Steve's offer to walk from north to south Goa over the course of four days, although I had not done any serious walking for years and even though I had no walking boots with me. I reasoned that walking was easy; what could possibly go wrong? We met on the Friday for a preliminary walk of a few hours around the cliffs and back roads from Baga to Anjuna. The walk was enjoyable and Steve told me tales of how Anjuna had changed; he had been visiting the area for over 30 years and had seen it evolve from a small village with local inhabitants and a few visiting hippies, to the busy little town it was now with almost as many visitors as native Goans. We climbed over the cliffs from Baga into Anjuna and passed the spot where a local Hindu man had decided to live on the cliffs above the sea and had built a small shrine to the gods Ganesh and Shiva. He was swimming in the sea below when we climbed past, but we saw the shrine and his bed roll and cooking pots. There was also a small pot and a sign asking for donations. Why anybody should wish to live on those rocks for years with no shelter was difficult to decipher, I wondered how he coped in the rains of the monsoon.

This trial walk gave me encouragement that I would cope fine with the four day ordeal. I had kept up with Steve no problem, happily scrambling up and down the cliffs and the time had passed quickly. I was looking forward to the proper walk, which we had planned to start on Monday morning; we would stay in cheap hotels along the way. We had arranged to meet early on Monday at a café in Baga where we could have breakfast together and then set off along the beach to Candolim. I had decided to walk to the café, which I reckoned would take around half an hour, a nice warm up for me. It actually took over an hour and I realised that the shoes I was wearing, cheap walking sandals, were not the most comfortable of footwear; I had blisters by the time I arrived at the café. We breakfasted and then set off along the beach to Candolim, I removed my shoes and walked barefoot in the sand. All was fine. On reaching Candolim a couple of hours later, we decided to have a coffee before hitting the road to Panjim, the capital of Goa, where we were staying the night. On reaching for my purse from my rucksack to pay for the drinks, I realised that I had left it in the café at Baga. Oh no! I had withdrawn all the money I needed for the four days accommodation and food and it was all in my purse, in addition to my credit and debit cards. I was so angry with myself.

I borrowed money off Steve and got a taxi back to the café, not really holding out any hope that the purse would be handed in. I figured out that I had left it in the toilet as I had gone there directly after I had paid for my breakfast, before setting off on the walk. I asked the taxi driver to wait whilst I ran into the café. Yes, they had the purse they told me and handed it over the counter. The money and cards were all there. Neither the customer who handed it in, nor the waiters, had taken anything. I was overwhelmed with gratitude and handed the waiters some money to share between themselves as a thank you. I arrived back in Candolim in the taxi and Steve and I set off for Panjim an hour later than anticipated, but with a strong feeling of faith in our fellow human beings.

We arrived in Panjim at around five o'clock and set about finding a hotel. The walk had been enjoyable and although my blisters were hurting, it was a manageable pain, not excruciating. I had easily kept pace with Steve and I was feeling confident about the rest of the journey. This was enjoyable, so far so good. The next day I was not feeling quite as euphoric. The thought of another eight hour trek in hot sunshine with feet that were sore and covered in blisters was not an enticing one. What I had not taken into account when agreeing to this trek was that my companion was a hardcore walker whose body was not only familiar with long treks, but who was dressed in the correct gear for such an excursion. No flimsy sandals for him! A few weeks after our adventure, Steve left for New Zealand to spend four months trekking in the wilderness; this was not a Sunday hiker that I was accompanying. He had little sympathy for my sore feet, which was probably the best attitude because, after all, what could he do about them? The day was agony though. I developed secondary blisters underneath my primary blisters and every step became a test of willpower. The second day was spent walking along tarmac roads that were so hot in the noon sun that the tarmac was melting; no taking off shoes and walking in the sand today. It was scorching hot, my backpack felt like it was full of lead and my feet were excruciatingly painful. It was a tough, tough march.

Even so, there were definite moments of reprieve along the way that eased the journey and made it worthwhile. The scenery and wildlife were breathtaking at times and transported me to another plane that left pain and fatigue behind for a while. We stopped to watch the most beautiful kingfisher with bright turquoise and red plumage that glistened in the sunshine as it landed on a fence post that we were approaching. It sat there for a few moments in all its glory and then flew off over the fields. Spellbinding. We walked past a lake that was overflowing with both blood red and creamy white lotus flowers, breathtakingly beautiful. My eyes gorged on the sight and it enabled me to downgrade my pain and discomfort for at least half an hour afterwards. The emerald green paddy fields were wonderful to see and so refreshing for the soul. Many times during the walk I was tired and weary, my blistered feet felt so painful and my legs and back were aching so horribly that I was near to tears wondering what the hell I was doing. However, something would occur which would lift my spirits and so I kept on trekking: A child waving from a car, a person greeting us as we walked past, a beautiful display of bougainvillaea, a refreshing cup of chai from a roadside shack. They were such small occurrences but they made such a huge difference.

Other highlights of the walk were when I was tired and weary during an ascent in the midday heat and suddenly two dogs came out of a garden and accompanied us for about a mile. One of the dogs was walking on only three paws and looked as though his leg was dislocated at the hip, but this didn't stop him from wagging his tail constantly for the sheer joy of being able to run in the sunshine with human company. As my companion said: "Look, walking's easy, you just put one foot in front of the other." If that doggy could run with a dislocated hip and still be full of joy, then I would damn well enjoy this trek with or without a few blisters, and so I did. On another day, we were trekking along the main road into Palolim, when two motorbikes came roaring along the road towards us being ridden by friends from Anjuna and so we had a mini reunion on the side of the road. Hugs all round.

In hindsight, I think I agreed to the trek to see what I was capable of; to see how much discomfort I could endure and, believe me, walking over hills during the midday heat with a heavy backpack is a feat of endurance. There was also a feeling that if I didn't do it then I might never have the physical capability to complete such a feat again; a kind of "use it or lose it" attitude. Anyway, I completed the task and felt rather chuffed with myself afterwards. I did opt out of the third day and caught buses as it was the most arduous day going over the mountain and I could hardly walk as it was. I had fresh blisters underneath my blisters, but I bravely popped these with a needle, taped them up, and carried on walking after my day of rest. It was a good feeling to know that my body was still capable of tough tasks.

On arriving back in Arpora I settled into my little apartment again glad of the rest. Steve had decided during our jaunt, to leave Goa and go trekking in New Zealand and so a group of us went out for a farewell dinner at a local restaurant. Relationships in Goa were transient; created easily and disappearing just as fast. People became superficially close very quickly, based on a shared understanding of cultures and customs that were alien to the country they inhabited. It was a fast track route to friendship that was just as easily abandoned when people moved elsewhere as they inevitably did. However, there was an underlying feeling of sadness when companions left, despite the brevity of the friendships. I was sorry to see Steve leave; I had enjoyed the trekking adventure we had undertaken together; he had been an ally when out and about at parties; he was good company and interesting to talk to. Another lone traveller with a tale to tell.

The next day, after Steve's departure, I felt the need for chocolate. I am not normally a sweet-toothed person, but in times of stress or melancholy I find myself craving chocolate. Just around the corner from my apartment was a rather handily placed supermarket. I use the term supermarket because this is what the shop called itself, however, in British terms it would be referred to as a corner shop. The assortment of chocolate was limited to a few bars of Indian chocolate and I chose the largest, a bar of hazelnut chocolate, perfect for murdering and burying melancholia. I rushed back to the apartment and put the chocolate in the fridge, as I did not want to eat it warm and sticky. I made myself lie on the bed for an hour, attempting to read a book whilst I clock watched the slow, slow passing of time. At the appointed hour, I rushed to the fridge and took out the anticipated bar. I unwrapped it slowly, broke off a large chunk of the rather delicious looking chocolate, and popped it into my eager mouth. Yuck! It was horrid. Over sweet, very greasy, and not tasting of chocolate at all. I tried another piece. Just as horrible. In disgust, I whizzed the remainder of the chocolate over the six-foot wall outside of my apartment and into the scrubland beyond. I went back to my book and became absorbed, forgetting all about my disappointment.

About an hour into reading, I was suddenly brought back to my apartment by a loud noise that I could not identify. It was a kind of snorting, grunting, slobbering, slurping, slavering sound at high decibels. I traced the noise to be emanating from the field in front of my apartment doors. I took a chair, placed it in front of the wall, stood on it, and peered over. There, on the other side, was the most enormous black sow who was slobbering over my chocolate bar wrapper. Saliva was dripping from her mouth as she was licking the wrapper clean of any stray crumbs of chocolate that may have inadvertently been left behind, and grunting with pleasure at the astronomical delicacy that she had just devoured. A small black piglet was standing beside her attempting to put his head beneath her to suckle, but she kept absent-mindedly kicking him away as she went about reliving her perfect moment. It was more than worth the torture of my disappointment to witness this thrill of chocolate heaven for another creature.

*

I soon became settled into the apartment and my previous feelings of loneliness dissipated. Not only had I made friends of my own to socialise with, but I was now comfortable with going out and about on my scooter and, also, I could relax in the apartment alone, which was impossible in the MamaNoo house. Life took on its own little routine. Every morning I would swim in the apartment pool, which was always empty. In the three months I spent at the apartment, I only ever shared the pool once with somebody else. It was a small swimming pool and I could easily swim across its length holding my breath, so I would try to swim 100 lengths every day, which took around 45 minutes at a leisurely pace. Wednesdays and Saturdays were taken up with the markets and we also hired a stall at Funky Friday's night market held at Hilltop, Vagator, for a few weeks, but this never really took off. During the day I would meet up with Nancy or Jean-Philippe or I would read or write or go to the beach to sunbathe and swim in the sea. Life was casual, easy going, and relaxed. I would often find myself riding along on my scooter with the warm breeze blowing through my hair and the sun warming my limbs, looking at the beauty of my surroundings and thanking the universe for all my blessings. Sometimes, whilst swimming in the pool or lay reading on the bed, I would recall that the day was a Tuesday or a Wednesday and think how far removed this was from my life a few months earlier and again thank the universe for my blessings. Life was good and long may it last. Amen.

Chapter 15: Phlipp-Phlopp

Joke: "What do you call a French man in sandals?"

Answer: "Philippe Philopp!"

I told Jean-Philippe the joke and he roared laughing, he had a good sense of humour and somehow after that he became known as Jean Philippe-Philopp and then just Phlopp. I do not think it dawned on him how others may have interpreted this! After the night of the dinner, post exhibition, Phlopp and I began to see each other regularly. We got on well together and shared a similar sense of humour. His interests in spirituality and in India were fascinating and he would tell me about the temples he had visited in order to sketch statues. On the main road to Arpora is a large bronze and peach coloured temple which is quite striking. I had told Phlopp that I had never visited a temple, and so, riding pillion on his bike one day, he stopped outside the temple at a coconut seller's stall. We bought coconut juice and then Phlopp suggested that we should visit the temple.

On entering the doors we came into an inner courtyard type building which had benches around the walls for people to sit on. There were a few people sitting down and Phlopp explained that it was common for people to come here to take rest and shelter from the sun. There was an inner door that led to the temple itself.

162

Phlopp reached up and rang the bell above the door as he entered the building and we went inside towards the altar that had a rail around it. Inside the rail and in front of an open door from which we could see a statue of Ganesh, sat the Temple Guardian. He offered Phlopp two flower heads and two bananas that were gifts from the temple. Phlopp went over to a stand and lit some joss sticks, waved them around to scent the air, and then placed them in a holder near to the alter rails. Not knowing quite what to do, I knelt at the rails and said a prayer. Phlopp then casually walked around the temple, closely examining the carvings on the marble walls, and then rang the bell again on leaving the building to enter the courtyard. It was all very peaceful, very beautiful, and very relaxed. We sat in the courtyard and ate the gift of bananas.

A Sadu, one of the holy men of India, was sat on a bench opposite and smiled at us; he joined his hands together in prayer and bowed, greeting us with "Namaste." We bowed and offered "Namaste" back to him. In broken English he asked us how we liked the temple. We told him that it was beautiful. He smiled. Nancy had told me that when she was in Mumbai she would quite often go into a temple to pray if she had any problems or troubles. She said that she found peace and solace through quiet prayer in the temples. I had asked if anyone minded her going there; I was unsure of the rules regarding Hindu temples and thought that a western woman alone may be frowned upon. However, she had informed me that lots of women visit the temples alone and everyone was always accepting of her or welcoming even. It appears that the Hindu gods favour anyone and everyone, which fits in nicely with my idea of religion.

Phlopp and I spent a lot of time touring the area on his scooter whilst I rode pillion. He was a confident rider and I felt safe with him. He knew the back roads to the local towns and so we usually went the scenic route to places. It was a warm, leisurely life, riding along on the scooter in the beautiful sunshine, eating out at cafés and restaurants, swimming in the warm sea, and jumping the waves. It all felt like an extended holiday. Phlopp too appreciated the life and would make comments about how very lucky we were to be here. He loved India; the land, the people, and the spirituality which was everywhere, even in the very air itself it seemed.

"Look around us, Jeel, oh my India eeez so beautiful."

*

Although Phlopp's English was good, he would get tired of talking the language and sometimes insist that we converse in French. The last time I had spoken French was at school many, many years earlier, so it was rusty to say the least. It did improve dramatically though in the three months I spent with Phlopp. He would text me in French too, which was frustrating as I was never quite sure if I had interpreted the message correctly, and if it was in regard to meeting up, I would have to text back in English to ascertain if I had understood properly. He did not always confirm. It reminded me of the difficulties that Hank must have endured on a daily basis. Hank was a friend of Phlopp's, an American who happened to live close by to my apartment and we would often go to visit him. He was always hospitable and welcoming to us. He had suffered a stroke the previous year and although, by all accounts, he had made a remarkable recovery, he still had problems with his memory and speech on occasions. He would forget what you had told him or grasp certain parts of the story and forget the rest. Likewise, he would mix up his words and substitute the wrong word in his speech, sometimes with hilarious consequences.

Hank was one of the rare visitors who lived in Goa throughout the year as he had a long-term visa. He rented a lovely apartment on a small complex about five minutes on scooter from my apartment. It was his birthday whilst I was in Goa and Phlopp had suggested that he have a party and offered to cook crêpes for the guests. We called round in the afternoon of the appointed day to visit and to check Hank's kitchen to see which additional ingredients we needed to buy for the delights Phlopp intended to create. Hank did not want us to go, asking us to stay now that we were there, but we had been swimming in the morning and needed to shower and change. We explained that we would just get ready, call at the supermarket, and then come straight back, as we realised that Hank was nervous about his party. He had invited around a dozen people.

We did just what we had intended to, but as it sometimes happens, real life got in the way of arrangements and we were held up at every turn. I forgot to put the water heater on when we entered the apartment and so we had to wait additional time for the water to warm up. It took longer than we thought to get ready and then when calling at the supermarket, we bumped into some friends of Phlopp and so were delayed there too as we chatted. When we eventually drove up to the gates of Hank's house we could hear that the party was in full swing.

"Oh no, my dear!" Phlopp shouted to me above the roar of the engine. "We will walk in late and zey will all be wanting zeir crêpes. You realise, *mon cherie*, zat zey weeell all theenk we are late because we aff been making love!"

For some reason the remark hit my funny bone and I could not stop laughing. I could just imagine walking into the room and everyone turning to face us, thinking what Phlopp had suggested. Tears were streaming down my face and I could not get off the bike for laughing. I eventually composed myself and walked up the stairs to Hank's apartment. Just as we were walking into the room, Phlopp whispered into my ear,

"Remember what zey will be theenking, *cherie*."

It was difficult to look anybody in the eye as I was introduced to them and I found myself over explaining to everybody exactly why we were delayed.

The party and the crêpes were a success and as we were leaving later on in the evening, Hank suggested that we visit an art exhibition in Panjim the following week. The exhibition was by a modern Indian artist and it was a tribute to the late American artist Jackson Pollock. We enthusiastically agreed. We met up at Hank's apartment on the agreed day and took a taxi to the gallery in Panjim. The exhibited art was neither to my taste nor to Phlopp's. In my opinion it was simplistic, talentless, and boring. All of the paintings looked similar and were of numerous small painted squiggles on various coloured backgrounds. I had seen children's art that was more interesting and required more talent. The prices of the work were on each piece and they were selling for the equivalent of thousands of pounds, many already had a sold sign on them. I felt the injustice of society as I was in awe of the beauty and talent of Phlopp's art and was also aware of the difficulty he had in marketing and selling his works. This just did not seem fair. I picked up one of the glossy brochures describing the work and containing a biography of the artist. He had been a successful advertiser before branching into the world of art. He had not had any formal training as an artist. No surprises there then!

After viewing his art works, the artist had arranged for an outdoor showing of a film about Jackson Pollock's life. It was fascinating and afforded an appreciation of the influence of Pollock's work on society at that time. The artist then pretentiously declared that he would now paint in the style of Jackson Pollock in front of this live audience. He had placed a huge canvas on the floor in front of the screen and began to cover it by throwing paint about in a dramatic, flamboyant fashion. After around half an hour of being the centre of attention, he declared that his 'Jackson Pollock' painting was complete. The mainly Indian audience were in raptures. I whispered to Phlopp inquiring if we were missing something here, I just did not get it. Neither did he. The audience was then invited to question the artist about his work and a show of enthusiastic hands waved in the air. The sycophantic queries were all in regard to how the artist had achieved his obvious talent. I sat there flabbergasted.

On arriving back at my apartment, Phlopp and I sat on the bed and chatted about the evening. I was still bemused by it all, especially the audience's reaction to the artist's work. It seemed like we were the only people there who did not appreciate it. I still had the glossy brochure in my bag and suggested that we read what it had to say about the art. I started to read out loud the brochure's description of the artist's work and was about halfway through the explanation when Phlopp let out a huge snort of derision.

"What a lot of bull sheeet!" he exclaimed, clearly exposing the Emperor's new clothes, and started to laugh.

I carried on reading, but it became hard to keep a straight face as I read out the pretentious gobbledygook that was written in the brochure. The more I read, the more we began to laugh until we were rolling around the bed holding our sides. Just as the laughter began to subside, I would compose myself enough to read another line and we would burst into peals of laughter again. The brochure had us in stitches for around an hour.

*

Soon after meeting Phlopp, he moved from his room in Vagator to Candolom where he rented some rooms on the top floor of a house. I quite often went over to his place, as the beach at Candolim was so lovely and had the most amazing shells that I had not seen anywhere else in Goa. They were small, delicate, and in pastel shades of cream, pink, and coral and, is if painted by hand, they had the most intricate pattern inlaid across the outside of the shell in a darker shade. The patterns had an Aztec look to them, being rows of 'V's and lines, for all the world looking as if somebody had painted these on. We both adored these shells and would collect them by the handfuls. Phlopp made bangles out of coconut shell as a hobby and would stick these beautiful shells, or sometimes semi-precious stones or pearls onto the outside of the bangles. They looked really good and he made me presents of several of these.

We both enjoyed swimming in the sea at Candolim as it was a little rough and the waves would come crashing into the shore. We were on the beach one day when Phlopp, ever the exhibitionist, declared that he intended to swim naked that day. The tide was out and it was quite a way to the sea from the shack where we lay on the sun loungers.

"And how are you going to do that?" I enquired. "Streak to the sea from here?"

"Exactly, my dear," he replied.

Then quickly removing his shorts, he dashed the hundred yards to the sea stark naked. I lay on the sun lounger laughing and watching the reactions of the other beach dwellers. I joined him in the sea later and he was extolling the virtues of naked swimming so much that I felt obliged to remove my costume whilst in the water to find out for myself. It was rather deliciously wicked.

"When I was small and I swam weeth my two brothers, we would often spot zee large white whale in zee water," he announced solemnly.

"Really?" I asked curious. "Whereabouts did you swim?"

"Oh, zee white whale can appear in any water, my dear," he retorted.

Then with that comment, he suddenly did a forward roll exposing his white buttocks for the world to see.

"Did you spot zee white whale, Jeel?" he asked on surfacing, a huge grin on his face.

"Yes," I replied, "I saw the large white whale and I spotted the little pink elephant too!"

169

He roared laughing and then ran out of the sea, butt naked again, and made a dash for his shorts that were still on the sun lounger at the beach shack.

We were still laughing about the white whale when we arrived back at his apartment. We walked up the stairs and stopped outside of his front door where he had placed a lock onto the bolt for extra security.

"Somebody 'az been tampering with zee lock again." he announced. "Zee numbers 'ave all moved around."

It was a numerical lock where, to open it, the numbers had to be placed in a certain sequence and Phlopp would only change one of the numbers when locking it for ease when unlocking later. The landlord of the apartment, Frances, an obvious alcoholic, lived in the downstairs of the house with his long-suffering wife, Angelina, and their teenage daughter. Phlopp had already complained to Angelina about the behaviour of Frances, as he would wander upstairs drunk and walk into Phlopp's apartment uninvited and without knocking first. He was an aggressive drunk too. The last time he had visited, he roared at Phlopp to turn his music off as he did not like it and it was his house. The music was only being played at a level where it could be heard in the apartment.

A few moments after we had entered the apartment, Frances came up the stairs and, once again, walked unannounced into the room. Phlopp, was pleasant with him and after greeting him, requested that he help him secure a hose for transferring petrol from his scooter tank into mine. Phlopp was exchanging his scooter due to engine problems and had recently filled the tank with petrol, which he felt loathe to give away to the extortionate scooter rental company. Frances declared that he had no idea where to get a hose and scurried downstairs again.

"Hmmmph, 'ee soon disappears at zee mention of vwork." Phlopp declared.

The scooter rental company were arriving in 30 minutes to take back the bike, so we had to act quickly if we wanted to keep the petrol. Phlopp decided to go downstairs and ask Angelina if she knew where we could get a hose. Angelina was obviously fond of Phlopp and had come to regard him as a confidante in the few weeks that he had stayed there; quite often popping upstairs when Frances was out, to discuss her worries about his drinking. Phlopp always listened to her patiently, realising that she just needed somebody to talk to.

Phlopp knocked on the downstairs door that was answered by Angelina. He explained the situation asking her if she knew where he could get a hose stating that he had already asked Frances, but that he did not know. Angelina smiled sweetly and announced that she would soon get us a hose. With that she turned to her husband who was sat watching the television and said something to him in Hindi, he immediately stood up and rushed past us. She then smiled at us again and made small talk until her husband returned in a few minutes with a length of hosepipe. She once again said something to her husband whilst scowling at him and then turned sweetly to us and passed the hose with her blessings. We thanked her and walked outside of the garden to where the scooters were parked under the frangipani tree. Phlopp lined the bikes up next to each other and then removed the petrol caps. He dipped the hose into the tank of his bike and then looked at me.

171

"Frances can suck oop zee petrol, I am not risking eet," he announced.

I did not see why Frances had to get involved in this petrol hustle as it was not his problem. I crossly took the hose from Phlopp's hand and started to suck. At that point in the proceedings Frances came out to watch what was happening. I carried on sucking and suddenly my mouth was filled with foul tasting, burning petrol. I stuck the end of the hose in my tank and spat out the petrol. My lips, gums, and mouth were on fire.

"Quick. Get me some water, I'm burning!" I yelled.

Phlopp ran off to get water and left me with Frances who started to laugh manically at my distress. What was so funny? I carried on spitting out saliva and petrol until Phlopp returned with the water and I swilled out my mouth over and over again until the burning sensation started to ease. Frances was still laughing. Phlopp pulled the hose out of my tank to check the petrol flow but it had ceased to run. We decided that the bikes were too near together and that mine was slightly higher. We rearranged the bikes and were ready to start the flow of petrol again. I noticed that Phlopp had now moved quite a distance away from the bikes and was busy fiddling with the two petrol caps. Frances still laughing walked up to the bikes, stuck the hose in his mouth, and sucked. Timing it perfectly, he removed the pipe just before the petrol started to flow out of the end and held it over my scooter. Petrol flowed into the tank. He was still laughing.

"Oh, Frances, thank you so much, you're a hero!" I said.

He laughed louder, then mimicked me spitting out the petrol and started his manic laughing again. He was still chortling as he walked back to his house.

"Ah, so Frances does ave eez uses," Phlopp announced, screwing the petrol caps back onto the scooters.

"I thought he was quite the hero," I said pointedly. "He might have found it funny when I filled my mouth with petrol, but at least he wasn't going to let me do it a second time." I declared, the inference being clear.

If Phlopp picked up on my disappointment at his unmanly behaviour, he did not acknowledge it, but entered the house muttering about how it was the first bit of work that Frances had done in a long time.

Whenever I saw Frances again after that incident he would start laughing at me and mimic spitting out petrol. He obviously found the behaviour of those strange foreigners hilarious.

*

Not long after the petrol incident I stayed over at Phlopp's apartment and in the morning he produced a breakfast of custard apples, a type of fruit which looks similar to an apple but with a consistency of custard when cut into, quite delicious.

After cleaning up the breakfast dishes, he suddenly announced brightly, "Zees morning, Jeel, we will meditate, it ees good for us!"

With that he put some meditative music on his computer and sat cross-legged on his mattress, which was on the floor as his bed frame was too small for his height and he could not stretch out. He patted the mattress next to him and I sat down. He shuffled around until we were both sat back-to-back cross-legged in the middle of the mattress.

"Now join in with me, Jeel," he instructed.

He began to chant in time with the music "Ommmmmmmmmmmmmmmm."

The chanting meditation lasted for around an hour. I fluctuated between acute embarrassment, discomfort, and a peaceful relaxation. When the music ended there was silence and we both sat there for a few moments.

"Well," I said, breaking the silence at last, "that's the first time I've ever meditated."

"Ow did you find it, my dear," he asked.

"Good, I felt a bit embarrassed at first," I confessed, "but I really got into it. I'll definitely be trying meditation again."

"Oh, my dear, there was no need for embarrassment," he reassured me. "Yes, we will definitely meditate together again."

We never did, although on returning home to England I took it up on a daily basis and now could not imagine my life without meditation, I have Phlopp to thank for that.

Chapter 16: Perfume Production

Phlopp, in keeping with his flamboyant personality, wore a perfumed oil instead of aftershave, it had a sharp, musky smell that was rather pleasant. On witnessing him patting the oil onto his neck one day, I asked him what it was.

"Oh, *mon cherie*, zees is geranium oil zat I meex with a leeetle base oil, you like, *n'est pas*?" I agreed that I liked it very much.

"Zen we will go on photo safari one day, my dear, and on zee way I will take you to zee shop zat sells zee perfume oils."

True to his word, Phlopp organised for us to go on a photo safari the following week, whereby we took our cameras and went for a long ride into the city and countryside taking photographs of whatever caught our eye. His love of India and Indian culture led to a fascination with the Indian way of life in all its diversity. He had thousands of photographs that he had taken during his visits to India, which he organised into various categories. He collected photographs of scarecrows, which were common features of Indian agricultural life; photographs of what he termed "sleeper," Indian people sleeping in various strange places, again quite a common sight in India with people working long hours in sunshine; photographs of "smilers," an array of Indian people smiling for the camera; photographs of people in various activities; and photographs of buildings, animals, landscapes, and seascapes. His artistic eye led to great photographs with good composition and amazing colours and angles; his collections were fascinating.

On arriving at Mapsa, the nearest town, he took me to the pharmacy store where he bought his geranium oil. The shop had a vast array of perfumed oils with a tester bottle for each perfume, so that customers could smell before buying. A notice informed that these oils were authentic, sourced from the plant in question, and were not artificially made like some of the cheaper versions produced. I was amazed at the range available and ended up buying around two dozen different oils with a base oil in which to mix them, and a score of little plastic bottles to put them in.

"You 'ave become a perfumer, my dear," Phlopp observed as we left the shop and it seemed that he was right. Back at my apartment I experimented with mixing drops of the various oils and when I felt confident with the fusion of smells, I mixed six separate perfumes, one each for Nancy, Phlopp, Emma, two of Nancy's friends who were staying with her at the time, and one for myself. Nancy came round to the apartment that evening as we were going out for dinner and so I used her as a tester for the perfumes. I placed a blindfold over her eyes, so that she would not see the name labels on the bottles, and then told her she had to guess which person I had mixed the perfume for. I allowed her to smell each perfume in a row, twice, and then when she sniffed each bottle again she was to state whose perfume it was. She scored six out of six. I was sceptical at first, thinking that she was cheating and could see the labels, but she insisted she could tell by the smell. Phlopp's perfume was quite masculine she stated, whilst hers was reminiscent of hippies with strong overtones of Patchouli oil, her friend Catherine's was quite sweet, and so on. I was amazed. Did I have a hidden talent for mixing bespoke perfumes or did she have psychic abilities, or both? Either way, we both got quite carried away over dinner with my perfumery, dreaming of selling these products on the markets and offering an online service, whereby I would take details of a person's personality and mix a perfume to suit. It was a best seller for sure. Sadly, our enthusiasm did not translate into action and the perfume business remains unlaunched.

*

Phlopp and I had been to Vagator beach one day and were contemplating going on to a local nightclub that evening. It was a club that I had visited previously with Kate and Nancy, and Phlopp also knew it. It sometimes had local bands playing fusion music, a mixture of eastern and western influences, which we both liked. Unfortunately, on arriving at the club, it was not live music, but trance that was being played that evening and so we decided to go home and watch a film instead. Just as we were walking to Phlopp's scooter, somebody called out his name and came strolling over. Phlopp introduced me to Luka, a friend of his whom he had known for several seasons and who was also French. They chatted in French for a while, Phlopp explaining to me that Luka spoke little English. I found French far easier to understand than to speak and so I listened along to their conversation. Luka was also staying in Arpora, in a hotel with his wife and eight year old son. They were here for six weeks of holiday. He invited us both to follow him to the hotel, and to spend the evening with them. We agreed and he roared off on his Norton motorbike with Phlopp anxiously trying to keep pace with him.

I knew the hotel when we arrived, it was one that Nancy and I used to dine at sometimes as it was handy being quite nearby to the MamaNoo House, even though it was rather expensive. Luka and his family's ground-floor room was simply lovely, with a veranda where we sat out, a huge bedroom, and a sumptuous bathroom that opened onto a small roofless enclosure with a huge Jacuzzi bath in it, enabling bathing under the stars. Luka introduced me to his wife, Marie, and their son Christoph. They were a particularly good-looking family and I felt fat and frumpy in comparison to his beautiful, elegant young wife, who was simply charming and very friendly; translating for me whenever the men spoke together in French. Phlopp did not know how they earned their money when I asked him later, but they were obviously quite comfortably off being able to take six weeks holiday in such a sumptuous hotel. It was protocol in Goa, never to ask anyone how they earned a living, as it was rumoured that in many cases it was the illegal drug trade.

Marie brought us beers and Luka told us about a new party drug he had sourced, stating how amazing it was. I was aware that Phlopp had taken recreational drugs occasionally in former seasons in Goa, although he no longer bothered. Marie agreed, telling us earnestly how she had partied until five o'clock that morning without once feeling tired and had then come home still wanting to dance, except that Luka had stopped her as he was annoyed at being woken up. They obviously took it in turns to look after Christoph. She looked so elegant dressed in a simple kaftan, without a trace of make-up on her beautiful face and her shiny, fair hair loose and flowing. It was hard to imagine her partying hard on drugs until the early hours. Never judge a book by its cover and all that. Luka then offered us some of the drug, assuring us that it was amazing and with no comedown afterwards. We followed him into the bathroom where he opened a wrap containing white powder that he tipped onto the sink surround, and then with a credit card, neatly arranged it into four even lines of white powder. He rolled up a rupee note, stuck it up one nostril and quickly snorted one of the fat lines, passing the note to Phlopp, who did the same. I followed suit, leaving the last line for Marie, who was obviously still in the party mood. We went back outside onto the veranda where we were joined by Christoph, who had been watching a film in the bedroom that had now finished. Unlike his father, he chatted away to me in excellent English. He was a charming boy.

The men spoke in French whilst Marie and I talked to Christoph in English. I could not feel any affects, whatsoever, from the drug and the only sensations I had were of hunger and mild tiredness as it was getting late in the evening. I felt myself yawning and noticed that Phlopp too was joining in. Luka asked us how we liked the drug, when Christoph went inside, adding how fantastic it was. I smiled at him nodding in agreement and noticed that Phlopp's response was equally lukewarm. We had not eaten and I was hungry and tired. I nudged Phlopp and made a slight incline with my head suggesting that we go, he nodded. After a few moments, we made our excuses, thanked them for their hospitality, and hugged and kissed them goodbye.

"What did you think of that drug?" I asked Phlopp as we walked towards the scooter.

"What drug?" he replied, "We 'ave just snorted 'alf a gram of talcum powder each, *mon cherie*, zat ees all." We burst into laughter that kept bubbling up from us both on the journey home.

I leant over to Phlopp's ear after he had let out another loud chuckle and asked, "How did Marie manage to dance all night on talcum powder then?"

"Zat ees zee power of zee mind, my dear, zee power of zee mind," he shouted back, over the roar of the engine, and we both laughed out loud into the darkness of the night.

We had not eaten since lunchtime and when we arrived back in Candolim, it was almost midnight with everywhere closing, as the season was now coming to an end. We rode around for a while searching for open restaurants, when Phlopp remembered somewhere that he thought might still be serving food. We drove down some back streets in the dark until we came to a little Tibetan restaurant where the lights were still shining, although when we parked up and walked in, all of the chairs had been placed upside down on the tables and a waiter was sweeping the tiled floor. We asked if it was too late to be served, but he just smiled serenely whilst pulling two chairs down from a table and indicated for us to sit down. He then walked over to the back of the restaurant, where the door to the kitchen was, and spoke to somebody there, presumably the cook, and came back to our table to take our order of momos, a Tibetan dish of dumplings.

Nestled Amongst Temples

As we were waiting for our food to arrive, I heard a slight gurgle and noticed a playpen in the corner of the restaurant situated under a picture of the Dalai Lama. When I went over to look, there sleeping comfortably, was a beautiful little Tibetan baby, smiling peacefully as he slept. The waiter smilingly came over with our food and I asked him about the baby. He proudly told me, with a huge smile, that it was his first child who was only a few weeks old. He and his wife owned the restaurant and also lived there, although the building consisted of only a small kitchen and the dining area. We had just arrived in time, he explained smiling, as his wife was getting ready for bed and he was cleaning up before retiring for the night also. I deduced it was his wife who had kindly cooked the food for us, which was absolutely delicious. Presumably the family slept in the dining area once the restaurant was shut. I wondered how they fared in winter when the raffia roof would afford little protection from the monsoon rains or perhaps they returned home to Tibet then. We tipped the restaurant owner well, after paying the bill for our feast, and thanked him profusely for his kindness in serving us when it was so late in the evening. He bowed his head with hands together in prayer, wishing "Namaste" to us as we were leaving, still smiling serenely.

*

The roads in Goa were extremely dusty and it was not uncommon to see riders without helmets, but with handkerchiefs and scarves tied over their noses and mouths to keep from breathing in the dust. I received a phone call from Phlopp one day, in which he told me in a desperate voice that he was "very eel. Jeeel, very eel." I drove over to see him and he was laying on his mattress, stark naked except for a scarf wrapped around his neck, coughing dramatically whilst holding his open hand flat against his mouth and his elbow raised in an exaggerated motion.

"Oh, my dear, I ham sooo eel," he moaned. "What can I do?" I suggested that I drove to the pharmacy and bought him some medication, to which he readily agreed. "I need zee antibiotics, Jeel, nothing else will touch me," he declared in martyred tones. I doubted that antibiotics would be of any help to him as it was probably a viral infection, but I did not want to dishearten him nor lecture him on antibiotic abuse. Most prescription drugs in Britain can be bought over the counter in India, so I drove to the nearest drug store and bought him a mixture of cough sweets, vapour rub, paracetamol, and antibiotics. He was pleased with the purchases, dosing himself up liberally and getting me to rub the ointment onto his chest, neck, and back whilst groaning dramatically. He was quite pathetic when feeling poorly it seemed and it was not the most attractive of traits.

By the next day, he declared himself to be no better and insisted that I gave him a lift to the hospital as he needed to be seen urgently by a doctor. I did as requested and went in with him to see the doctor who sounded his chest and then prescribed antibiotics, paracetamol, and cough mixture, advising that he may also wish to purchase vapour rub. It was an almost identical prescription to mine, being the same antibiotics the pharmacist had advised me to buy. The effect on Phlopp, however, was little short of miraculous. "I feel so much better now that I aff seen zee doctor, Jeel, see 'ee 'as prescribed for me the correct drugs and I will now get better," he faithfully announced.

It was well over a week before there was any improvement in Phlopp's cough though making me think that it was viral after all. Following on from this episode, Phlopp became convinced that it was dust from the roads that had settled onto his chest and made him "so 'eel." He took to wrapping a lungi, a large Indian scarf, around his nose and mouth whilst he rode, and because it kept slipping, I was tasked with holding it in place. This did not work when I was not there, of course, so, instead, he made himself a mask out of several layers of sheet material and elastic. It was huge and covered half of his face, so that it was like riding pillion with the Lone Ranger whenever we travelled anywhere, but it seemed to keep him happy and certainly made me smile. He was becoming more eccentric by the day; a trait not just reserved for the British I noticed.

Chapter 17: Holi, Holi, Holi

The Wednesday Flea Market had become quieter as the season crept on and quite often we would find ourselves sat around the stall bored as tourists became fewer in numbers. Both Nancy and I had become friends with Adrian who ran a bookstall on the market, situated at the end of our row. He was British, about 50, and had a shock of curly ash-blonde hair and John Lennon style glasses, quite attractive in a casual, not-trying sort of way. He looked quite youngish and had a friendly demeanour, being chatty with most people on the market. He stayed in a room just behind the bar where the market was held and kindly offered us storage for our table and chairs, to save us from carting these to and fro each week. Nancy became very friendly with him, going over to chat whenever the stall was quiet. He sold an assortment of second hand books and lent these to us at no charge. One of the books he lent Nancy, *Goa Freaks,* was written by one of the original hippies who arrived in Anjuna in the 70's. It was a popular book amongst the foreigners living in Goa, as many of the places it mentioned were still popular venues. It was rumoured that some of the people described in the book were the older hippies who still frequented these places and whom we had met on several occasions. Nancy started to read the book one day at the market, and when she went to buy lunch I picked it up and also became enthralled. As I loathed giving it back to her when she returned, I offered to read it aloud. It became a weekly ritual to read from the book whenever the market was quiet. We were both fascinated by it and would discuss it in between readings. The book contained pictures, one of which was of the house Cleo, the author, had rented and renovated whilst she lived in Anjuna.

Whilst on the beach one day with Nancy, we were discussing the book and decided to try and find the house. We walked up and down the beach for around an hour looking at the houses in the vicinity of the book, but nothing compared. I kept being drawn, however, to a house that was presently being renovated, with a cement mixer and workmen's tools in the front room, visible from the open door. The picture in the book showed the top half of a detached house with no other houses around, although this house had houses close by on either side, only separated by a few metres of land. Also, the windows of this house, although similar in shape and design, were in different positions to those in the picture. I stared and stared at the house, trying to figure out why it was that I thought this could be the right one, when it suddenly dawned on me that we were misconstruing the picture.

"Look, Noo, this picture isn't the front of the house, it's taken from the side," I declared. "See, the windows on the side of the house in the picture matches the front ones of this house."

"No, it's a different house, Mama," Nancy insisted. I was unsure, however, as something was niggling at me.

"The houses on either side could easily have been built at a later date and that's how the picture was taken from this far away. Let's take a look inside, the door's open."

We walked into the house, shouting "hello" as we did so. A workman appeared in the doorway smiling. We told him that we were looking for the house in our book and showed him the picture. We asked could we look around. He smiled obligingly obviously not able to speak much English. I was feeling unsure if this was the right house after all, as the front room just did not match the description in the book. However, as soon as we walked into the next room we knew that we had found the Cleo's house, because the staircase that she had designed and described in great detail in the book, and included pictures of, was still there and had not been ripped out with the renovations. It felt strange to walk around the house and see the places and imagine the happenings that Cleo had described so vividly. The author had died since the book was published and we felt as though we had been compelled to find the house to corroborate Cleo's existence. The memory of her life, gained through reading the book and viewing the house, felt so near, almost as though we had experienced some of these memories for ourselves. We were both subdued after the viewing, lost in thoughts of how fragile life was.

*

Nancy's friendship with Adrian, the bookseller, continued until it finally dawned on me that the relationship was more than friendship. I was not overly pleased as Adrian was much nearer to my own age than Nancy's and I felt that she was quite vulnerable, having come out of a long-term love affair prior to her travels to

India. She seemed to be hell bent on choosing relationships that were doomed for disaster since that time. I was not in a position to say anything to her, as she was old enough to make her own decisions and I did not want to fall out with her about this. My silence around the matter spoke for itself however, and she tackled me about this and we ended up rowing anyway. They were both from different generations and to make matters worse, she informed me that Adrian did not want children and had undergone a vasectomy when he was much younger. When I asked her how she felt about this, I was informed that it suited her as she did not want children either. It was only a few weeks previously that she had been bemoaning that she may never find her life partner and, by the time she did find him, she may be too old to have children. She had changed to suit Adrian and I was worried for her, but she perceived my care as negative and interfering; we were so similar in disposition and spent so much time together that we ended up clashing about almost everything these days. I decided, however, that my relationship with Nancy was too important to scupper over a man, and so I arranged to meet up with her and explained that I absolutely loved her and did not want to fall out any more. It cleared the air and we ended up hugging with Nancy telling me that, although she really liked Adrian, she did not envisage the relationship lasting after India. So, theirs was also an extended holiday romance, just as I perceived Phlopp's and mine to be. I felt relieved, for although I liked Adrian, I did not think he was right for my beautiful daughter.

Nancy invited me to join her in celebrating the festival of Holi in Mapsa the following day; she was going with Adrian and two girlfriends who were staying with her. She warned me to wear old clothes, which I did not mind throwing away afterwards. I had heard about Holi, the festival of colour, and readily agreed to the outing, it sounded fun. We met at Nancy's house the next day and the two girls rode pillion on Nancy and Adrian's bikes whilst I followed behind them and, in convoy, we rode to Mapsa, about a 30 minute ride away. We parked the bikes in the town centre, which was already heaving with people covered in powdered paint of luminous colours. Within minutes, people were running up to us and showering us with the powdered paint. We bought some bags for ourselves off a street seller who was also paint smothered, and commenced our attack on each other and anyone else in the vicinity. It was great fun and before long, it was difficult to make out who was who, as we were covered from head to toe in colour. Adrian's curly hair had been showered with bright orange powder, which resulted in his curls turning to frizz and sticking out like an afro, and then somebody attacked him with a handful of scarlet powder turning his face bright red. With his t-shirt by then covered in green paint and his trousers and shoes in purple; he looked for all-the-world like a clown. We were in hysterics until we saw the photographs of ourselves.

We wandered along the busy streets to the park where sprinklers and hoses were turned on and people partied to the music, dancing under the water and turning their bright coloured paint to a murky brown. It looked fun, but the thought of riding home in dripping wet clothes was not appealing and so we had a drink at the bar and then left the park in clothes still dry. On the way back to the scooters, we stepped over a man who was fast asleep on the pavement, which was not in itself an

188

uncommon sight in India, but there was something about the way he lay in the middle of the pavement, in the blazing sunshine, that was unusual. He was covered in paint, but had a trickle of red coming out of his ear. I stopped, bent down, and shook him gently, saying "hello, hello," but he did not respond.

"Leave him, Mama, he's just drunk" Nancy said, obviously embarrassed by my behaviour.

"I don't think he's just sleeping," I said, feeling the sticky, red substance oozing from his ear. "I don't think this is paint."

Just then two Indian men came up and looked at him too, they were also covered in paint. "No, he is sleeping off the drink, madam," they said, "that is just paint coming from his ear." They sounded convinced and so I got up and walked on with the others, but I noticed that Adrian kept looking back at the man.

"I think he's unconscious, Adrian," I said. "I'm sure that was blood. Let's go back and check, we can't just leave him." Adrian came back with me, obviously concerned too. We shook the man and spoke to him, but there was no response. It was definitely blood coming from his ear.

"We need an ambulance." I said. By good fortune a police car was just driving past and Adrian stepped into the road to hail it down. By this time Nancy and her two friends had returned.

"No, don't get the police involved." Nancy screamed. "They will just beat him up, you don't know how it works in India." She protested.

"But he hasn't done anything." Adrian muttered as two policemen came over to us and we showed them the man. They were driving a Range Rover type of car and they opened the back door and placed the seats down ready to lift the man inside, stating that they would take him to the hospital. They both picked him up, but it was like carrying a sack of potatoes, he was a dead weight and sagged in the middle, Adrian and I ran to assist. The man did not move or respond at all. He was deeply unconscious. His shoe dropped off on route to the car and Adrian ran back to retrieve it and placed it beside the man. The police waved as they drove off. I suddenly remembered how we looked, a clown and his rainbow assistant, I was glad that the police had taken us seriously. As we started to walk back to the scooters, a group of Europeans stopped us to ask what had happened. We recounted the occurrence.

"Thank God it was an Indian," one of them remarked.

"What the hell has that got to do with anything?" I retorted furiously.

"He didn't mean it like that, Mum," Nancy barked at me as we walked off. "You took that completely the wrong way." She was clearly annoyed with me for making a scene.

"How did he mean it, Nancy?" Adrian asked quietly.

Nancy didn't reply, I think she was embarrassed by the whole incident, but especially my part in it. The atmosphere had gone from carnival to morose and we walked back to our scooters in silence, it had been a sobering experience, but one in which Adrian had risen dramatically in my estimation.

*

Nestled Amongst Temples

Holi carried on for several weeks after this outing, moving from village to village, so that almost every time we went out on the scooters, we ended up being showered in colour. The fun of Holi began to wear a little thin, as the paint took days to wear off I discovered when my chest and neck took on the appearance of the god Shiva—a bright luminous blue. One evening, after treating myself to a rather expensive silk blouse that I had coveted for weeks, I wore it to go out to dinner with Phlopp and got covered in purple paint on my way to his apartment. The blouse would not wash clean and was ruined. I ended up throwing it away and wearing one of Phlopp's shirts instead. Not really the look I was hoping for. Unfortunately though, this was not the end of the trials of Holi.

Nancy arrived at my apartment one evening quite hysterical and covered in green paint. She had taken the shortcut to my complex through the back roads and, near to a temple, had been attacked by a group of around 12 men, who blocked the road she was driving down, so that she had to stop her bike. It was dark and nobody else was around; she was terrified and screamed at them to go away. They all ran towards her at once, a huge laughing pack, grabbing at her and covering her in paint. She could smell the alcohol on their breath. She was petrified that she was going to be knocked off her bike and raped. Some were groping up her skirt, some her breasts, whilst somebody else had climbed on her bike and was hugging her from behind. It was a terrifying ordeal. Luckily a car drove up the road at that point and the pack moved away from the middle of the road, so Nancy grabbed her chance and roared off. We discussed calling the police, but realised that there was little point as she could not identify any of the men as it was dark and it had all happened so quickly. We avoided shortcuts after that incident and stuck to the busier main roads when travelling at night. Overall, Holi turned out to be a lot less fun than I had imagined.

Waiting for the train to Delhi in Margoa Station, Goa
Nancy at the train station in Margoa, Goa

On the train to Delhi

Baba on the train across the tracks — somewhere between Goa and Delhi

Baba coming across the tracks with his present

Delhi from a rooftop restaurant

Head covered to visit the Golden Temple (Gurdwara Bangla Sahib) in Delhi

Nancy and me about to enter the Golden Temple

Ox drawn cart — Delhi

Jillain McKay

The Lotus Temple — Delhi

Nancy on the train journey from Delhi to Ajmer, near Pushkar

196

In the gardens of the guesthouse in Pushkar, Rajasthan

Pushkar from a rooftop restaurant

Chapter 18: The Creature from the Deep

Nearby to Phopp's apartment was a bookstore that also doubled as a coffee shop. It was situated in a magnificent, old Portuguese house, the grounds of which were large and very pretty being filled with flowers and frangipani trees which left a lingering fragrance in the air. It was a popular haunt of Phlopp's and mine and we happily lingered over coffee whilst browsing through the enormous selection of books on offer, many of these art books, which we both enjoyed reading and commenting on together. I had mentioned the bookshop to Nancy on several occasions and she was longing to visit, as it was one of the few venues that I had experienced, but she had not. One day, we took a ride together to the bookshop, and after browsing through the books, we ordered coffees and sat in a swinging seat in the garden admiring the plants. We had decided upon an afternoon at the beach, and, whilst waiting for the bill to arrive, I announced to Nancy that I would visit the toilet.

Now, the toilets in India are quite an interesting phenomenon and one that I kept threatening to write a book about, for tourists visiting the area, giving each a *loo rating* with marks out of ten. For conversely it was quite often the most up-market joints that would achieve a low loo rating and vice versa. The nicest toilets that I had encountered on my travels; ones that had fresh, clean toilet bowls and seats, clean sinks with working taps, paper towels, working lights and doors, and plenty of toilet paper (a rare treat indeed), was at a very basic Indian café in the busy centre of Margao in Goa. It was a venue not geared for tourists at all. I had mentally rated these particular toilets a nine, achieving an extra point for the uber trendy stone sinks that they sported, although I did realise that it may have been coincidental that this functional design was also bang on trend.

The toilet at the bookshop was outside in the gardens and of brick built construction, with a corrugated roof and a wooden door painted a dark green to match the house. It was quite a roomy toilet and no smell hit me as I walked into the room, which was always a good sign; in fact the room had air vents to allow for fresh air to circulate and it smelled quite sweet. So far, so good. It was the type of toilet that one could comfortably linger on after breakfast to complete one's ablutions in relative peace and comfort, knowing that nobody was waiting to come in, as there was nobody else in the shop; and so that is exactly what I did. Whilst I sat there, I mentally rated the toilet a six, it was clean and fresh, but lacked towels and toilet paper, although I had long ago learnt to carry a fistful of paper serviettes with me when departing for the toilet in restaurants. I had not had Delhi belly for the first month of my travels without learning something.

After leisurely attending to my toilet, I carefully wiped myself with the fore mentioned serviettes and then stood up to flush the bowl. To my absolute horror and mortification, a large black lizard-like creature ran from inside the toilet bowl to hide under the rim. I screamed inwardly and flushed the toilet quickly, it darted its enormous head out from under the rim as I flushed, its sly green eye staring at me ominously from its side vantage point. This disgusting creature had been gawking at my bits, I realised. I charged out of the toilet at full pelt running over to Nancy, screaming inwardly and cringing outwardly.

"Whatever's the matter, Mama," she asked with concern when she saw my face. I told her the tale amidst much squirming, shaking, and cringing. Nancy burst into peals of laughter.

"Oh, Mama, do you think the creature from the deep was already lurking in the bowl, or do you think it could have crawled out of your bottom?" she asked innocently with a grin gaping across her face from ear to ear.

"Oh God, Noo, what a disgusting thought. Of course it didn't come out of my backside! Eeewww, don't even go there." But it was too late, the damage was already done and the image of my arse giving birth to that alien creature was indelibly etched into my brain. Thereafter, the whole of the afternoon was spent trying to think of more pleasant images, with little success. I was extremely nervous of Indian toilets after that experience, and lingered on them no more than was absolutely necessary and I point blank refused to sit down on a toilet seat again, preferring to perch precariously above them in order to avoid any razor-like teeth.

*

The Wednesday Flea Market had become so quiet towards the end of the season that we decided it was not worth doing any more. This just left the Saturday Night Market, which was still very popular with both Russian and Indian tourists, no doubt because of the party atmosphere. Both sets of tourists seemed to have plenty of money to spend and it was just a matter of attracting them to the MamaNoo stall, which was, fortuitously, situated near to one the several bars scattered around the market. An Indian lady and her husband walked into our stall one night, she stood in the middle of it demanding to see one of the bags. We took the bag in question down from the shelf for her. She put it over her shoulder, moving it this way and that, barking orders at us about where we were to move the mirror that we were holding in front of her to allow viewing. Then she tried another bag and then another. After around 30 minutes she had ordered us to show her every bag in the shop, noticeably, she had not said please or thank you once. Eventually, with nothing more to look at on the shelves, she alighted on the bag Nancy had over her shoulder and was using as a moneybag. "I want that bag," she announced.

"But this is my bag," Nancy said. "This is my personal bag."

"Just let her see it, Noo," I whispered. I had a feeling that this was the sort of woman who would only buy something if she knew that she was depriving somebody else. Nancy reluctantly took the bag off her shoulder and gave it to her, pointing out that there was a very similar one on the shelf that she had already tried.

"How long have you been using this bag?" the woman demanded.

"Oh, she's only used it tonight," I interjected quickly, "It's a way of advertising our goods."

"Then I'll take it," she said.

"She only wants it cos I've got it, selfish bitch. We should charge her an extra thousand rupees," Nancy muttered to me under her breath, as she emptied her belongings from the bag and wrapped it. It was rather obvious that this was a woman who was used to getting her own way.

Unfortunately, Nancy had not removed all of her belongings thoroughly and, true to form, she discovered after the customer had gone, that she had left her mobile phone in one of the bag's pockets. She used my mobile phone to ring it, but nobody answered. I suggested that she send a text and give my number, which she did, but we heard no more from the woman that evening. The next day, I received a call from a man saying that he had the phone and asking where he could drop it off. I was having coffee with Phlopp at the time in Candolim, so I explained where I was and asked if this was a convenient spot, I was told that it was. About 20 minutes later, a man in a smart chauffeur's uniform came up to me and returned Nancy's phone. It seemed that our MamaNoo bag had moved allegiance to the "have lots" from the "have nots"...we definitely should have charged that extra 1,000 rupees.

*

The Saturday Night Market was a dressed up affair and we always made a special effort when working there, wearing party clothes and gaily painting our faces as an advertisement for the face painting service we also offered. We were friendly with lots of the stallholders and regulars who frequented the market, and although it was hard work, it was also lots of fun. We were regular customers ourselves for some of the hawkers who walked around the market selling their wares. There was

"Johnnie Chocolate" who made and sold the most amazing dark chocolate, all made from organic ingredients, he assured us. He did not turn up every week and sometimes it was several weeks before we saw him again, rumour being that he liked to party hard. We always bought a good stock from him when he came around, just in case we did not see him again. Another favourite of ours was "Camembert Chris" who was a fromagier and made the most delicious cheeses. He was a British man who had retired after years in the navy, married a German lady and started a life in Goa. They had permanent visas and lived in India all the year round. On arrival in Goa, he had found that retirement bored him and so he learnt how to make cheese, which started as a hobby and had since become a passion. He made a variety of different cheeses including buffalo, mozzarella, and gorgonzola. Quite often I would buy a piece of cheese from Chris, take a nibble before I put it away, and then within half an hour I had devoured the lot, just by having another little taste and then another. It was outstanding cheese, but not only were his cheeses great, he had a lovely, friendly personality and we got on well together. His wife was petite and very pretty, flouncing around with him in gorgeous floaty skirts and dresses, very feminine. She must have been around late 40's or early 50's in age, but still had the tiniest waist and prettiest face; they were such a lovely couple. When his wife was visiting Germany he came around to the stall unaccompanied and we chatted for quite a while, before he went on to his other customers.

"You make me cringe the way you two flirt together," Nancy announced to me after he had gone.

"We don't flirt, Nancy, we're just friends," I said rather hurt, but it left me pondering on my behaviour. I concluded that Nancy was wrong though, we were not flirting, but being friendly. We obviously liked each other, but it was not in a physical sense, I just thought he was a lovely person and I was interested in him and his life and he in mine. That loving exchange between two people who genuinely like and are happy to see each other had been misinterpreted by Nancy as flirting.

Not such a friendly person, but definitely a character, was Marco, a large Italian man who had a stall selling vintage sunglasses. His age was indeterminable; he could have been anything between 30 and 60 years of age. He had thinning hair that was tied into a greasy, thin ponytail and he was a rather small man with a huge beer belly. He was always sweating in the heat. Nancy had met him on previous occasions and she came back to the stall after buying a drink one evening and told me about a pair of gorgeous sunglasses she had just seen on his stall. "He's quite a character, Mama," she had added, "You should go over and meet him." His stall was not far from ours, so I strolled over to say hello. At the time, some customers were at his stall admiring his display of glasses, one of the customers picked up a pair.

"Geddya fuckin' hands offama fuckin' sunglasses," Marco screamed at him. "You don't toucha the fuckin' goods 'tilaya fuckin' pay for them." The customer walked away quickly, obviously mortified. Marco looked at me, "And that goesa for you too," he added venomously.

"Hi, Marco, I'm Jill, Nancy's mum. She said to come over and say hello." His expression changed immediately and his frown was replaced by a beaming smile.

"Hi, Nancy's momma, lovely to meetaya." He held out a sweaty hand and then kissed the back of mine. "Try on any of the glasses you wanta, I just don't wanta these fuckin' morons breakina them. They come to my fuckin' stalla, trying on everya fuckin paira. They drive mea fuckin' mad." His customer service skills lacked a certain finesse, I noticed.

Marco had been married to a Goan girl, who also had a stall on the market, and he was another of the few foreigners with a permanent visa. Unfortunately, a few years after the birth of their daughter, the pair split up and the relationship between the two parents had turned sour, with neither speaking to the other. Marco told anyone who would listen, how she had only married him for his money and how she had bled him dry. His wife, whom Nancy pointed out to me with his daughter one evening, seemed much younger than him, although he may have looked older than his years. The little girl was four years old and absolutely beautiful with her dark, wavy hair and huge brown eyes, if nothing else good had come from the relationship, they had created the most beautiful child. We would see her at the night market most weeks, running between the two stalls of her mother and father. Marco often brought her over to have her face painted, which she loved. He obviously adored her and was very proud of her, telling everyone in the vicinity that this was his little princess. Towards the end of the season, however, the little girl had started to ignore her daddy, no longer speaking to him, obviously influenced by her mother. He called out to her one night as she came running over to our stall to have her face painted. She totally ignored him, even when he left his stall to come over, stand by her, and say hello. Nancy and I both had tears in our eyes, as he walked back to his stall, head down and dejected; then we heard him roaring at the next customer who stopped by to browse. It was heart-breaking.

*

Nancy had declared one day that she was going to travel north to source stock for the next season. She was considering branching into designing clothing and jewellery instead of handbags, as these had proved bulky to move around and expensive to send home. Adrian was travelling north for a week before flying home from Delhi, so Nancy intended accompanying him and staying on an extra week. This left me to cover the last market alone. We discussed taking a taxi to the market with all the goods for ease of transportation, and paying coolies to transfer the bags from the taxi to the stall. We had used coolies in the past and they were not expensive, but when you are on a tight budget every rupee counts, so they were an occasional treat. Besides, the last time we had used coolies it had resulted in a fight between the women. There was a pleasant young girl, who was amazingly strong despite her diminutive size, we would sometimes pay to carry our bags up the hill to the stall if we were feeling tired. Otherwise, it meant one of us waiting by the bikes whilst the other person carried one load, left it at the stall asking one of our neighbours to keep an eye on it, and then went back down for the last large load that we carried between us. If we hired the coolie, she could easily carry the suitcase on her head whilst hauling another bag over her shoulder, whilst we carried the rest. The women would wrap a piece of cloth into a doughnut shape, place this on their heads and then place the load on top of this. They had amazing balance, marching up the hill to the stalls with the loads on their heads hardly moving, it seemed a point of pride between them not to steady the load with their hands.

We hired this particular coolie one evening when we arrived and promised her that she could also help at the end of the night. She was cheaper than the other coolies as she carried more bags for the same amount of money, although we always tipped her extra. There were lots of Indian women who worked as coolies on the market and as you drove into the car park they swarmed over to the scooters and cars, like wasps around a cream cake, all vying to carry the loads on their heads to the stalls. It was the same at the end of the evening too. When we came to pack up this particular night, coolies appeared to help us, but we told them that we already had one booked. Our coolie, however, did not appear, presumably busy on another job. After waiting a while, we asked two other coolies to help and just as they had placed the bags on their heads, the girl we had booked arrived. There was an almighty row between them, with other coolies coming over and joining in. One of the women pushed our young coolie in the chest who in return pushed her back harder. In the end, Nancy broke up the fracas by screaming at them that we did not want any coolies if they could not behave and to go away. She started to take the bags off the two women's heads, who had been balancing them throughout the fight. It all left a sour taste in our mouths as far as coolies were concerned.

207

I was not looking forward to covering the market stall on my own while Nancy was away, it was time consuming putting the stall together and dismantling it in the early hours of the morning, when everyone was tired and longing for bed. Tough enough with two of us, but on my own it would take real effort. Phlopp kindly offered to help me when I told him, saying that he would call at the market during the evening and stay to help me dismantle it all. I was very grateful to him and thanked him profusely. I took a taxi as arranged and arrived early on the last night of the market, it was heaving with people. The coolies helped me to carry the stock to the stall and I paid one of them extra to help me arrange it all. The stall was ready in record time. It was a busy night, with no let-up. Neighbours watched over the stall as I nipped to the toilet (a mere two on the *Loo Rating* scale) and bought a sandwich and drink, but this was my only reprieve all evening. Phlopp arrived about ten o'clock when the market was in full swing. He kissed me on the cheek and then spread out a lungi in the middle of the floor, sat down, took a flask and two glasses out of his rucksack, and announced wearily, "I 'ave brought us gin and tonic, my dear, so zat we can get drunk. It ees zee only way we will get through zees evening." I was a little surprised by his behaviour, not least because I did not think of him as a drinker, never having seen him partake of more than one beer, and that only on the odd occasion. I had to admit, though, that this seemed like a plan and a rather attractive one too. So I sat down and joined him with his flask of ready-made gin and tonic. He had brought a lime with him too, which he sliced and added to our drinks. "I am sorry, *mon cherie*, but I did not 'ave a way to carry zee ice." Good as his word, we sat and got drunk.

As we were blocking people from walking around the stall being sat plonk in the middle, customers stayed away, which suited me just fine. I had earned the money at the start of the evening, and as an added bonus, when I had gone to pay the weekly rent at the beginning of the market, I was told that as we had paid a week in advance, there was no charge for this last market. So I gaily downed my gin and tonics, quite guilt free. Regulars bobbed in and out of the stall to chat to us, some even joining us on the mat for a short while. We were both in good spirits by now (literally), laughing and bantering with passersby. At midnight I decided to pack up the stall, although we usually waited until at least two in the morning, often not arriving home until four a.m., but as I was not trading anyway, I decided to pack up early. Phlopp started to help me and then became bored, "I theeenk I will go 'ome, my dear, I am feeling quite tired now," he said with an exaggerated yawn. I was shocked, so much for his help. There were no coolies around as they did not appear until later, and so I had to struggle alone, making three back-breaking journeys to the car park, loaded up with stock. I sat down on the bags after the last journey and started to drunkenly sob, as I waited for a taxi. One of the guards that I had asked to watch the bags noticed that I was crying and sauntered over to me to ask what was the matter. I told him my drunken tale and he gave me a big hug and the wise words, "You should never cry over a man who is not kind, madam. There are too many kind men in this world who are far worthier of your tears." At that point my taxi arrived and he helped me to load my bags into it. "Take care, madam," he called after me, waving as the taxi drew away. The kindness of strangers. Now there was a man worthy of tears.

I was still angry and hurt when I arrived back at my apartment. The small complex always had a security guard on duty, and at night they would sit in a little sentry box in the car park outside of the gates, to allow people entry to the villas and apartments. I normally carried the bags and boxes to the apartment myself after the markets, although the guards always offered to help. Tonight though, throwing thrift to the wind, I accepted the young man's offer of help. Feeling quite merry, I asked him if he had a cigarette he could give me. I have never really been a smoker, but if I smell cigarettes when drunk I always crave one and he had been smoking as the taxi pulled up at the gates. He offered me a cigarette and lit it for me and then I wished him goodnight, carrying my bags up the steps and through the doors of my apartment. Inside, I sat on my bed still feeling dejected and blue. I suddenly remembered seeing a bottle of cognac in one of the cupboards, left by the previous tenants, so I got it out and drank it, mixed with lemonade. It was half full when I started and completely empty by the time I had finished, but I did feel a lot happier. I remember little else about the night, save going back out to the sentry box and spending it talking and smoking with my guard friend. Goodness knows what I was saying to him as we perched together in his little hut, but ever after that night he would beam whenever he saw me and offer me a cigarette. As I was never drunk again, I always smilingly declined.

"Why does he always offer you a cigarette?" Nancy asked me one day as we walked through the villa gates.

"Oh, I bummed one of him one night when I'd had a few drinks," I explained, omitting any details. There are some things better left unknown when it comes to the behaviour of parents.

Chapter 19: Comings and Goings

In addition to Josie, Ade, and Otis visiting for two weeks in the New Year, a dear friend, Penny, whom I have known since my school days also visited for a week in February, with her two daughters. She had visited me with her husband when I lived in New York over thirty years previously, it seemed that it was turning into a tradition. They stayed in a hotel about a 15 minute walk away from my apartment and we spent most days together on the beaches and dining out in the evenings. It was nice to show my friend the places that I frequented and I would invariably bump into somebody I knew when we were out together, making me realise how established I had become in such a short space of time.

Unfortunately, at the time of their visit, Nancy and I were at our most volatile and were constantly bickering about everything. Not least because it was nearing the end of our time in India and savings had dwindled, so we both had to be careful with our money. At that time, because Nancy had previously lost her purse and cash card, I had withdrawn a series of cash transactions for Nancy, which she transferred electronically back into my account from hers, although according to my calculations, she was one transfer short of around seventy pounds sterling, and according to Nancy, she had paid up. Despite me printing off the bank statement and demonstrating to her the short fall, she was adamant that she had paid all that I had withdrawn for her; she was wrong though and I was furious about it. For one thing, I did not wish to be the keeper of the purse, it was a nuisance having to ride out, at Nancy's request, to the one ATM machine in the area, which was in Anjuna a 20 minute ride from my apartment, and then drop the cash off at Nancy's house. I would end up lending her small amounts of money when I was out with her, and then have to keep reminding her to repay me the next time I saw her, to be told, of course, that she was certain she had already done this, or to make sarcastic comments to me about my thrift. I kept asking her to request another bankcard, but as her bank was in England, and rumours abounded about Indian mail being opened, she did not trust that the card would arrive safely. She would, however, have had time to contact the bank and arrange for Josie to bring the card out with her, but she did not get around to this, and so I had to continue as banker, although I loathed doing it.

There was an unspoken resentment on Nancy's part around money where I was involved, almost as if she thought that I should pay for her, like when she was a child. She would make veiled references to my money status with the inference that I was being mean or selfish with her. When I tackled her about this, explaining that I had no more money to spend than she did, she would state that I had a job to go back to in England and she did not. She seemed to think that I owed her a living despite being 30 years of age; it was a regression to adolescent thinking. I was not really sure how to tackle this and, as always, it ended up as bickering, with one or other of us storming off. As the saying goes though, blood is thicker than water, and we did not hold grudges for long and would soon become friends again. We were both of similar dispositions, fiery and volatile, which made for a fearsome combination when forces were joined, but equated to fireworks and big bangs whenever we clashed.

Nancy and I arranged to go out to a beach party one night with Penny and her daughters, so that they could experience for themselves Goan trance music, which I had told them about having had a strange experience with this music. I had been out to a party one night with Nancy and friends and was feeling rather bored, stood around the bar watching the dancers and listening to the same interminable beat of the music played at ear shattering pitch. I suddenly decided to dance and had submersed myself into the music, shutting my eyes and swaying in time. After a while I "awoke" to the fact that I was on the dance floor, but I had completely lost sense of how much time had elapsed being locked into the beat of the music with few other thoughts entering my consciousness. It seems that this style of music with its relentless, repetitive beat can prevent normal thought processes from occurring and thus allow for transportation to other dimensions, akin to deep meditation or hypnosis—hence the name, trance. I rationalised that my boredom and tiredness that night had assisted with the process, for I had not touched alcohol, or any other drugs for that matter, although on telling Nancy and friends, she teased me mercilessly that I was "tripping out" on the dance floor. I could imagine, however, that plenty of people at these raves were chemically aided to this state though, if their beatific expressions and strange behaviours were anything to go by.

Nestled Amongst Temples

On arriving at the beach party with Penny and girls, we fought a path to the bar for drinks and then made our way to one of the omelette sellers on the beach to sit down on their mats, away from the heaving crowds and the loud volume of the music. Penny found that she enjoyed trance, standing up after a while and dancing on the beach. Her daughters were amazed, commenting with astonishment at their mum's obvious enjoyment of the experience and teasing her about this.

"They don't seem to recognise that I was once a teenager or in my 20's," she confided to me. "They just see me as always having been their mum. For God's sake, why shouldn't I like this music?" she queried. It was almost a relief to witness tension within her family too, and counterbalanced the spats between Nancy and myself a little.

*

I had told Phlopp that my friend was visiting from England and invited him out to dinner with us on a couple of occasions, but he either declined or made an excuse at the last minute and did not turn up. I was left feeling puzzled and hurt as I had told Penny about him and she was looking forward to the meeting. In the end, I decided that he could do what the hell he pleased, but that I was spending time with Penny and family, who had travelled all this way to see us, and so that is exactly what I did. When Phlopp next contacted me to ask to meet up, I informed him that I was spending the week with my dear friend who had come to visit me, and although he was very welcome to join us, I would, otherwise, be unable to meet with him until the end of their trip. This take-you-or-leave-you attitude seemed to spur him into action and he arranged to join us at their hotel that afternoon, where we planned to lounge by the pool. We had a lovely afternoon and he and Penny got on well together and she seemed quite taken with him, commenting that I had over exaggerated his flamboyant and effeminate manner and that he had an attractive personality. She invited him out to dinner the following evening, which was their last night in Goa and he willingly agreed to join us. I did notice that he was not as dramatic as usual in her company, which was interesting, although I had no answer as to why this should be.

We dined the next evening at a superb restaurant that both Nancy and Phlopp had recommended and that I was longing to try. Phlopp called round at my apartment prior to the ride to the restaurant, as it was quite nearby, although he insisted that we go on separate scooters, whereas normally he loved me to ride pillion behind him so that we could chat as we rode along. I did not think too much about this at the time, reasoning that he might be a little concerned about having a drink of wine and then being responsible for me riding on the back. So I took my own scooter and followed him to the restaurant, which turned out to be as good as reported and we spent a glorious evening under the stars whilst the food and wine flowed and the laughter spilt over.

Not long after Penny and her daughters returned to England, the weather in Goa began to turn, becoming extremely hot and humid. The locals nodded sagely whenever I mentioned this, telling me that "the monsoon is coming, the monsoon is coming." Where, previously, I had hung my damp towels outside to dry in the sunshine for an hour and then brought them back in crisp and dry, now they could stay outside all day and still remain damp. Mosquito bites and small cuts took weeks to heal, I noticed, as skin stayed moist in the humid atmosphere. People were constantly mopping their brows. We had a few days where big fat raindrops splashed onto the parched earth heralding the rains to come; it was the first time I had seen rain in India.

As the weather changed, people who were staying in Goa for the season began to pack up and, either go back to their homelands, or travel on elsewhere. Emma had left Goa to visit Nepal with Pierre, and some of our other friends had also gone travelling. Nepal and Ibiza appeared to be favourite haunts. A photographer friend of ours from the night market was desperate to get home to England with her two children, but had run out of money, and she was hoping that her mother would buy her the tickets. It seemed that everyone was on the go. Holidaymakers too, were not visiting the area in the numbers previously seen and the formally bustling little village of Baga, near to where I lived, now resembled a ghost town. Everywhere had a different feel to it without the people, even the beaches and shacks became deserted and we quite often found ourselves sunbathing with nobody else around us, unimaginable earlier in the season.

We also noticed a change in the street dogs as the season became quieter, they were normally so docile and friendly, but had begun to turn nasty of late. On rides out with Phlopp in the evenings, packs of them would chase the scooter down the dark lanes, yapping and growling at our feet. "I fucking 'ate zem, zee bastards," Phlopp would scream as he kicked out at them whilst revving the bike to get away. It was the same when I returned home from

217

the Night Market on a Saturday, loaded up with goods, and it was a scary experience with five growling dogs snapping at your feet as they chased the bike down the dark lanes whilst I swerved to avoid them. I began to dread riding out at night. A friend of ours, who had worked at an animal sanctuary in Goa, informed us that the dogs turned aggressive at this time of year as there were less people around to feed them and less scraps left lying about for them to scavenge. These were hungry creatures and they were baying for blood.

Many of the restaurants kept cats to keep the mice and rats at bay and the German Bakery, next to Nancy's house, had a cute little tabby kitten, which played enchantingly with the customers. The German Bakery was one of the first restaurants to shut down as the season neared its end and the poor little kitten had been left to fend for itself. It made its way over to Nancy's house wailing pitifully and she had taken it to the little shop on the corner to buy it some food and ask the Indian shopkeeper what she should do with it, as we were soon leaving the area too. The shopkeeper shrugged wearily and told us that this happened every year, adding that it was not just the Indian restaurant owners who left their animals when the season ended, but also the tourists who visited the area and adopted cats and dogs and then left them to fend for themselves when they packed up and left. It was all such a pitiful state of affairs. Nancy fed the little mite those last two weeks before we left to go travelling, desperately asking anyone who was staying if they would care for it, but to no avail. She refused to let it come into her house as she wanted it to become independent and to hunt for itself, but we doubted it would survive.

Nestled Amongst Temples

Phlopp was leaving Goa almost two weeks before Nancy and I started our travels and he too was travelling up to Delhi as he was flying home from there. We went to the travel agents together to book our train tickets. I was expecting him to ask me to travel to Delhi with him and to meet Nancy there, but he did not. I reasoned that as he was going to spend two weeks touring the temples of the region to make sketches for his paintings, he would be busy and feel beholden to me if I was with him. We loosely arranged to meet in Delhi when I arrived, ten days later, a couple of days before he flew home.

The night prior to his departure we dined at a lovely Italian restaurant where he bought me dinner, which he had never done previously, as we always went Dutch. He had sold some of his paintings that week and was feeling pleased with himself, although he hated the selling process feeling like a carpet salesman, he confessed. I also bought a painting off him that week. It was the first painting I had seen of Phlopp's, the picture of Ganesh that was hanging in the doorway of the house when we arrived at the viewing, months ago. I had immediately loved it and although I had asked to buy it from him on several occasions, I think he felt embarrassed charging me. Eventually though he did and he presented it to me that evening along with another painting of the face of a serene Buddha that he had first sketched in a temple in Karnatika. He painted in a stippled fashion, which gave the appearance of age to his paintings in keeping with the age of the statues that inspired him. They were quite beautiful. He had placed my canvases into two wooden slats at the top and bottom of the picture in order to hang them then he had rolled the canvases up and placed these into cardboard tubes ready to be sent home. He gave me the painting of the Buddha first, stating that he wanted to give me a painting before he sold me one. I was rather hoping that he would not charge me for the Ganesh painting now that I had ordered it, as it was weeks ago that I had offered to buy it from him and I was becoming rather worried that my money would not eke out. He took the money from me though, much to my chagrin as I realised that, had the tables been reversed, I would have freely given the painting to him. He was leaving dozens of paintings in storage in Goa and he would arrive next season with dozens more, having been in his studio all summer painting. I was also aware that he had given numerous paintings away to his friends as presents, he had told me as much and I was with him when he gave Hank a birthday present of a painting, which was ungratefully received with, "Oh not another painting." So I felt resentful when it came to actually paying for mine. There was a temptation to order the most expensive food on the menu in recompense when he announced that he would buy the meal, but that was churlish, and I had offered to buy the painting on several occasions, I realised.

We went back to stay the night at Phlopp's apartment as he was leaving first thing in the morning. I felt a strange mixture of emotions. I had enjoyed his company over the last three months, we had got on well together sharing the same sense of humour, but I was not in love with him, nor him me. We had not shared the intimate confessions of lovers whereby every secret is spilled out and every tale told, late into the night. I knew little about his past life, save that he had been divorced for several years and his wife had worked as a curator in a museum. She had been dissatisfied with his lack of

fame and consequential lack of fortune. He had no
children, but had brought up his wife's son. Likewise he
knew nothing about my past life, apart from the fact that I
divorced when the children were small and had two
daughters and a grandson. I found it quite refreshing at
first that we did not discuss the past, although I did
sometimes wonder if it was a barrier to intimacy. We
never discussed what would happen to us once we had
both returned home either, whether we would visit each
other, although Phlopp was keen that, like him, I should
return next season.

   That night I could not sleep. We had ordered a
bottle of Italian red wine at the restaurant, but Phlopp had
only drunk a small glass of this and I had finished the
rest. Although I was far from drunk, my mind was
whirring and I just could not settle. We went to bed and
Phlopp was soon fast asleep and snoring, but I was still
wide awake. The moon shone through a small chink in
the curtain providing a slither of light to the pitch black
room. There were no street lights in the area, so once
shops, restaurants, and houses turned off their lights the
night became an inky black, lit only by the stars and
moon. I considered getting up and riding home, but it was
late and I did not want to disturb Phlopp who had to be
up early for his taxi and, besides, it was probably our last
night together. So I stayed where I was, staring at the
moonbeam and contemplating my time in India.

   At some point in the early hours, I turned over
onto my side facing Phlopp who was turned away from
me. I was still wide awake and I rested my head on my
hand as I lay on my side. I looked over at him trying to
make out his shape in the darkness as my eyes adjusted,
having been staring at the shaft of light. He was sleeping

221

with just the sheet over him as it was so warm and this was now pulled down to his waist. As my eyes focused I began to make out ghostly shapes, like whiffs of smoke, standing out from his back and head. I was shocked and could feel my heart pumping with fear. As I stared, I saw that the shapes were lotus flowers each with various numbers of petals, continually opening and closing. The flower above his head was quite spectacular with hundreds of petals that continually closed in on themselves as new ones opened behind, like an inwardly revolving doughnut. I realised that I was seeing his chakras, the seven openings situated along the spine in eastern philosophy. I was awake all through the night and continued to see the chakras until dawn broke and the room was flooded with light. I got up with Phlopp and we embraced and then, with tears in my eyes, I left him when his taxi arrived, and rode home on my scooter. I did not tell him about my vision.

When I got home, in the peace of my apartment, I pondered on what I had seen. The rational part of my mind told me that I had drunk too much wine, I was very tired, the room was dark and I was emotional because somebody I cared for, and had just spent the last three months with, was leaving and I may never see him again. I had probably fallen asleep and dreamt the vision. In my heart though I knew that this was not the case, and for some strange and weird reason that I could not fathom, I had seen the chakras. If I had recounted my vision to a local person, they would have accepted it at face value and would not have been in the least bit surprised or doubting. Western culture just did not allow for spirituality I reasoned, constantly demanding evidence and proof. I researched chakras on the internet to be told that the seventh chakra is known as the many petalled lotus which correlated perfectly with my dream. India is renowned for its spirituality, it is everywhere, buried, no doubt, in the very earth itself. It would be hard to live here and not be touched by the mystical nature of this wonderful country and its people. The conditions that night were conducive to visions and so the gods blessed me with a sixth sense for a short while. Ours is not to wonder why.

Chapter 20: Goodbye Goa

In the last two weeks that Nancy and I were in Goa we started to pack up our belongings that we had accumulated over the last six months, it was amazing just how much we had collected. Some of this we intended sending home to England and the rest we discussed putting into storage, as we were both considering returning the following season. Nancy had taken with her most of the furniture, soft furnishings, and kitchenware that we had accumulated in MamaNoo House as her new apartment was barely furnished. Even though my little apartment was well furnished, I had managed to gather lamps, ornaments, bedding, wall hangings, crockery, towels, clothes, toiletries, and a collection of books. It is surprising how quickly possessions mount up. Nancy had all of the belongings that she had brought with her from Mumbai too, as she had been in India for well over two years now, and she announced that she was going to be ruthless in sorting through her possessions, only taking home to England what was absolutely essential.

I started to sort through my belongings, earmarking them for one of three piles, those that were being stored in Goa, those I was parcelling up and sending home, and those I was packing to take with me. I ended up with three roughly equal piles. By all accounts, the mail service was quite reliable, albeit slow, when posting parcels home. I collected cardboard boxes from the supermarkets and boxed up my belongings for home, fastening it all securely with rolls of duct tape. I took the parcels one by one, as I packed them, to the main post office in Candolim, attaching the large boxes to my scooter with bungee ropes. The first time I went, I was told that I needed photocopies of my passport and that the parcel had to be bound in cloth and that, next door, was a service offering this. I found a shop to photocopy my passport and took my parcel to the little hut next door to the post office for the wrapping service. There, a man who could only be described as a tailor, was expertly cutting white canvas cloth to fit the size of the boxes concerned and then in record time, neatly sewing the box into a snug fitting canvas jacket. I studied his needlework afterward he had completed my box, and it was sewn superbly, with tiny, almost invisible, stitches evenly all the way round. Apparently when sending parcels home by sea, which was the cheapest route, boxes often split open due to the rough handling and thus the jackets protected contents from being spilt and lost.

As the cloth wrapping service cost almost as much as the postal service, I decided to wrap the other three boxes myself. I had some pale coloured sheets that I cut up to use, but although the tailor had made this look so simple and easy, it was actually quite tricky to accomplish. My box jackets were skewwhiff and baggy, with huge pleats in places where the material was clumped together as I had sewn it unevenly elsewhere. Nonetheless, they did the trick, although I noticed that the man behind the post office counter had a wry smile on his face every time I handed over one of my hand sewn parcels.

There were plenty of other jobs to attend to as well before we left. The stall at the night market had to be dismantled, as we had paid a builder to construct this because the stall had consisted of only four small bamboo poles marking the spot. The builder had constructed the actual stall with huge bamboo poles, adding a sloping roof of plaited reeds over these and steadying the whole construction with cross poles of bamboo, all bound together with thick twine. We had then sewn black cloth to the dividing wall between our neighbours stall, strung lights from the ceiling, with lampshades also made from black cloth and painted our bamboo poles in gold. We fastened bamboo matting to the floor. With our black and gold MamaNoo signs hanging on three sides of the stall, it looked quite striking. We would be able to use the poles and roof again next season and so we spent a sweaty morning dismantling it all and transporting it in an open backed rickshaw to Nancy's house.

Nancy and I spent most of our time together during these last two weeks in Goa, as the majority of our friends had moved on. She stayed over at my apartment quite often and we discussed where we could store our belongings, which included the art cards, and materials, which had not all been sold or used, and were too heavy to send home. We thought perhaps Santosh, our ex-landlord, may let us store our belongings at MamaNoo House, as we had been informed by Burma that it was still empty. We phoned him to ask and he told us that he intended renovating the house during the monsoon, but that we could store our stuff in one of his guesthouses, for a fee. We arranged to take it over to him the night before we left. I went round to Nancy's house the last week to help her to sort everything out; she had accumulated so much stuff that there were bin bags full of clothes and toiletries to be given away. I suggested that we leave them in one of the temples to be distributed to the poor, and we thought this a good solution. We bought tin trunks from the market and travelled home with these tied to our bikes to store the rest of our belongings. We had an assortment to store consisting of our merchandise, chairs, stools, kitchen utensils, pans, crockery, cutlery, lamps, bedding, towels, ornaments, wall-hangings and the dismantled market stall consisting of bamboo hanging rails, wooden signs and shelves, and, of course, our beloved chair. Nancy's little spare bedroom was stuffed full of belongings ready to take to storage.

As the house was emptied Nancy realised that it needed a good clean and called round at Burma's house to ask her if she would assist. Burma readily agreed and Nancy returned with Burma riding side-saddle on the back of her scooter, Indian style. When Burma saw the huge pile of belongings for storage her face lit up and she asked us what we were doing with these. We explained that we were putting them into storage for next year, for when we came back again, however she bustled up to the two red plastic chairs, beaming at us and asking, "Can I have these?" We told her that we would need them for next year, but this did not deter her and she asked again at least three times. Eventually Nancy and I went out and left Burma to her cleaning and then Nancy gave her a lift back home afterwards.

*

As the weather got warmer, the bugs seemed to grow larger, to our horror. My apartment was relatively bug free, apart from my old enemy the ants that were able to crawl under the patio doors. I more or less solved this problem by applying a chalk, which was available to deter ants, liberally along the top of the three steps leading up to my apartment doors. I had to remember to do this every few days though, as it was soon blown away. As my bed doubled as a sofa, once pulled out it was quite close to the floor and the thought of these huge ants getting into bed with me was abhorrent. I could imagine that they gave nasty bites too. They really were Jurassic, unlike their dwarf cousins back home in Britain. They had also got into my bathroom, presumably through the drain, so I chalked all round the drains and pipes in there too, and all round the window frames, just to be sure. I would shuffle to the toilet in the early hours of the morning, open the door, turn on the light, and there to my horror would be an army of ants crawling all over the floor. It really was like something out of a horror film.

One of my neighbours, Charlie, who had also declared war on the ants, informed me that shaving foam was a wonderful deterrent. He squirted it along the entrance to his villa. And, according to him, the ants were unable to breathe in it and died. He took me to see one of the ants' nests one day, at the side of the villas; it was high up in a tree, a huge sphere shaped object, a rusty red colour. Two battalions of ants were marching parallel to each other, in opposite directions, along the top of the six-foot high villa wall, onto and from a low hanging branch, up and down the trunk of the tree and into and out of their nest. "We should chop off that branch," I suggested, "that will maroon them." My neighbour laughed. Apparently, Goa had a terrible problem with ants, and buildings and houses regularly crumbled because of their invasions. Cath, my neighbour at the villa and at the Night Market, had told me that there were a couple of villas at the complex and the apartment above mine that had been left empty for many years, as people had bought these, but never used them. They had terrible problems with ants one year and Cath suggested to the villa caretaker that they look into the empty villas and apartment to check they were all right. When they opened the door of the apartment above mine, it was crawling with ants and termites, which had eaten through cupboards, wardrobes and even the plaster on the walls; apparently they had made a nest inside the fridge, which had been left open to allow the air to circulate as the apartment was empty. People had to be brought in to clean out the apartment and fumigate the buildings.

I was swimming in the pool one day, when Charlie came out of his villa and warned me that it was quite dangerous to swim that day as there was a huge hornets' nest on the villa wall next to it. I got out of the water and he pointed out the nest, which he said had appeared almost overnight. It was a large, black, cone shaped nest, clinging to the top of the villa wall. Huge wasp-like creatures were swarming around and buzzing in and out of it. "Listen," Charlie said, and as we both kept still, a clear droning noise could be heard. I noticed several of the huge insects flying near to us. "They're coming to remove it tomorrow. Stay indoors until then," Charlie warned me. "I'm going to watch them do it," he added, grinning, he obviously had a fascination with insects.

One of the last evenings we were in Goa, Nancy was staying at my villa, when as we entered through the patio doors in the evening, a huge insect flew in with us and landed on the wall above the bed. It was a flying cockroach and absolutely enormous. We stared in horror, knowing that it would have to be caught before we could go to sleep. I got a large glass from the kitchen and steeled myself, but it flew to the top of my high walls, out of reach even when stood on a chair. "We'll just have to go to sleep and forget about it," was Nancy's suggestion, but I knew that sleep was impossible with that beast out there, flying free. I was contemplating knocking it down with a broom handle, when it suddenly dived, amidst much screaming and shrieking, and landed on the floor near to the bed where we were sat. Quick as lightening, I plonked the glass down over it; captured. Then we slid a card under the glass and took it outside to set it free, so that it could live on, to torment some other poor, unfortunate soul.

*

On one of our last evenings in Goa we visited Chapora again. It was one of the little towns further inland from Anjuna and a popular drinking spot for many of the long stay tourists. It was a strange little town, consisting of one main street with a few shops and stalls, a juice bar, one small bar and another central bar, quite small, with a veranda that opened up onto the street. It reminded me of a Wild West saloon when sat drinking there, as it had the same vibe, but instead of cowboys on horses going past the bar, it was hippies on motorcycles. The younger hippie could be seen everywhere in Goa as could the older, original version. The young ones were usually thin, sported dreadlocks, often with one part of their head shaved; they had plentiful tattoos and wore dark green, dark grey, or black clothing with leather waistcoats and feathers in their hair and plentiful brass jewellery. It was a definite uniform. We referred to them as the "feather and leather brigade." We became friendly with quite a few hippies on the markets, they were usually transient, just staying a few weeks and then moving on. Many of them made and sold jewellery and would rent temporary stalls. Jewellery was light and easy to carry and, if it was the plaited string type that was popular for bracelets and anklets, it did not require tools, as they would simply hold the string between their teeth as they plaited. They would spend the day smoking spliffs, making their jewellery, and chatting to friends, an amiable laid-back bunch.

Lots of hippie types lived in and around Chapora, as it was much cheaper to rent rooms and houses there, being a distance from the beach and the main tourist spots. It was rumoured that a lot of the older hippies, who had become addicted to drugs, lived here and that mafia types ruled the town. According to rumour, there was a truce with the local police and the long standing addicts who lived here, and as long as there was no trouble and the inhabitants were discreet and stayed away from tourist spots, then the police would leave the area alone. Whether this was true or not, was difficult to know, but it did seem that several addicts lived in and around this region and there were some very strange and sad souls that you would bump into when on a night out there. As the town only had a couple of bars and both of these were small, it was impossible to go there for a drink without talking to other people, as you would invariably have to share a table with others.

I visited Chapora twice, both times with Nancy, and they proved to be interesting, enjoyable nights. The first time we chatted to two male friends, one from Holland and the other from Belgium, they were both a little drunk and quite hilarious, teasing each other mercilessly. The second time we visited, just before we were leaving Goa, we chatted to a Dutch man and his daughter and some Englishmen, one of whom had just arrived in Goa that day and another who was drunk and making a total nuisance of himself to everyone around. There was a kind of dark undercurrent running through Chapora, which we were more aware of on our last visit, perhaps due to the rumours we had heard. It felt as though there was something happening that we were not party to, but that we would keep catching a slight glimpse of throughout the evening. Lots of older, rocker types frequented the bars and they all seemed to know each other; they were in their 50's and 60's, once good looking although now faded, they were skinny and wore jeans, with long hair and they all seemed to smoke heavily. Someone would pull up outside of the bar on a motorbike and sidle up to one or other of the rocker cowboys at the bar or on the veranda, and then they would go outside together around the side of the veranda and return a while later, whilst the other sidled back to his motorbike. Spliffs were openly smoked at the bars, and even chillums were smoked in dark corners with people shouting "Boom Shankar" before they inhaled it and passed it on. So, whatever was going on with the cowboys, it was a little more sinister than hashish or weed.

The Dutch man was friendly and chatty telling me that he was staying in Chapora for four months, and that his daughter had arrived to visit him that week. He had sold an engineering business and had spent the last two years visiting Goa for six months of the year, he was mid 50's and continually rolled and smoked spliffs for the two hours we were chatting, although he remained articulate and I could not detect any effect on him. During our conversation, he told me that he had experimented with Ketamine a few weeks ago, but that it was an experience he would never repeat. He informed me that after taking it, he had watched a large ant crawl up his bare leg and under the shorts he was wearing, but as he was relaxed to the point of immobility, there was nothing he could do about it. It sounded like a living hell, the stuff of nightmares. As my friend's daughter had commented when I repeated this tale back to them, "Ketamine? Just say neigh!"

*

The night before we left we hired a truck to take all of our belongings to Santosh's guesthouse for storage. Although the truck was large, by the time we had filled it with our stuff it was packed full, so much so that there was no room for us up there with it. "Let's leave the chairs and take them to Burma's," Nancy suggested and I readily agreed. We followed the truck on our scooters and at the other end, we paid the taxi driver, then unloaded it all into one of Santosh's little apartments that he rented out. "Have you fastened it all up well?" he inquired. "Otherwise the rats will eat it." Nancy and I looked at each other and tried not to laugh. Not the best advertisement for his guest houses, which he was always asking us to promote to our friends.

We returned our scooters to Santosh too as we had rented these off him when we moved house, and had arranged for him to take us back to our respective homes by taxi. We were both going back to finish the final packing and then Nancy was coming round later to stay over, as we had a taxi picking us up in the morning to take us to the train station in Margao. By midnight she had still not arrived and I was getting worried, she was not answering her phone. Just then she turned up with numerous bags and her sewing machine which she was taking travelling with us; so much for essential items only. She told me that she did not have time to drop the bags of clothes off at the temple, so as she was dropping the red plastic chairs off at Burma's on the way, she also dropped the four huge bags of clothes and other stuff off with these. The lights were not on, she told me, so she had just left these outside of the front door. Burma would know they were from us because of the red chairs.

"What was in the bags?" I asked curiously

"Oh toiletries, washing up liquid, that sort of stuff. Plus a load of my clothes, shoes, and jewellery that just wouldn't fit into the case. Mini skirts, shorts, vests, tops, dresses..."

We both looked at each other as she was speaking and the thought hit us both simultaneously. "I can just imagine Burma the next time we see her, horned into one of your mini skirts with a racer back vest on and a load of beads hanging around her neck." The suggestion brought a vivid picture to mind of little plump Burma kitted out in Nancy's gear, and we both burst out laughing. After that, when on our travels and Nancy was searching for an item and then bemoaning the fact that she must have left it behind, my standard reply became, "Never mind, Noo, just think how nice it'll look on Burma."

Nestled Amongst Temples

*

I was sad to be leaving Goa and saying goodbye to that chapter of my life. For all I was contemplating coming out again next season, I knew that this would mean giving up my job and career, selling my house, and saying farewell, again, to my other daughter and grandson for another six months. I did not really know if I could do this, or if I really wanted to. The last task I undertook whilst in my little apartment was to write a note to Phlopp. I had bought some lovely cards with the face of Buddha in gold on a deep red background, quite striking. I did not have a purpose for buying them, but vaguely thought that they would make a nice little present for somebody. As I came to pack them, I took one out on a sentimental whim and sat down at the table and wrote to him. I told him how much I had enjoyed his company, but how I did not know if I would come out to Goa next season or, indeed, if I would ever see him again. I wished him well in his life. As I did not have an address for him, I wrote the address of Joe Banana's on the envelope, and then I strolled out to the guard at the front of the building and asked him if he would post the letter for me the next day, I gave him money for the stamps and his trouble.

Joe Banana's was one of the original cafes that opened in the 60's, when the hippies first arrived in Anjuna. It featured heavily in the book that Nancy and I had read at the day market and I was longing to visit it, but it was tucked away from the beach and notoriously difficult to find unless you knew it. So Phlopp took me one day and we lunched there; they made the most gorgeous fresh juices, the gooseberry being a particular delight. We spoke to the proprietor who was the son of

Joe Banana, who had since passed away. I asked him about Cleo, the author of the book I had read, and he told me he remembered her and that "she was just some junky who hung around." I noticed that they sold her book though and another book on Anjuna, as both authors had advertised the cafe well. Phlopp showed me the mailbox that was mentioned in the book, as Joe Banana had allowed the original tourists to use that address to have letters and parcels sent to them and so the custom continued with present day visitors to Goa. I had laughingly said to Phlopp that if I did not arrive next season, I would write to him at Joe Banana's to let him know. I did not know if he would remember this incident, but there would be a letter waiting for him if he did.

That last week, as I rode along on my scooter in the beautiful sunshine or swam in the frisky Goan sea, I tried to imprint it all on my memory. I was so grateful for my time here; for all its ups and downs, I had made it and come out laughing. I had lived on my own in a strange country, far from home, with a completely different culture and set of customs, I had made friends and carved out a path for myself, but more than all of that, I had come to love it. I knew that this had been a special time in my life and one that I would always cherish.

Chapter 21: Delhi — 72

The train from Goa to Delhi took two days and I had booked first-class sleepers. Nancy was rather annoyed with me for this extravagance as she informed me that the second-class sleepers were perfectly adequate, especially with our limited budget. Besides we would miss the gypsies, she informed me, who boarded the cheaper carriages banging their drums and singing for the passengers. Second-class was not the cheapest tickets we could have bought either, as there were also third-class tickets that did not include bunks although the thought of two days travel without lying down, was dreadful. The trains were well organised and ran efficiently. Our train would take us straight into Delhi with only a few stops on the way. There were four bunks in each carriage, two bunks at each side and another single bed next to the window by the aisle. They were roomy enough to sit up on or lie down. Clean bedding, including blankets, sheets, and pillows, was placed in paper bags on each bunk. There were curtains to draw across the bunks for privacy. The windows had glass panes and the carriages were air-conditioned. It was very comfortable. Our journey was inclusive of food and drink, three meals a day with a cup of chai. The food was amazingly good considering the industrial scale of the catering and the tiny kitchens they had to work in. All meals were of Indian cuisine consisting of vegetable curries, lentil dhal and chapattis with salads, and an Indian desert. They were served in tinfoil dishes and were tasty and enjoyable and helped to break up the long interminable journey. We looked forward to their arrival. We slept, dozed, read, thought, and listened to music to pass the time. My bunk was on the aisle and Nancy had the bottom bunk in a carriage, so although we were close by and could see each other, we had to shout across the passageway if we wanted to converse.

We eventually arrived in Delhi and paid a porter to carry my suitcases and Nancy's largest bag up the station steps to the outside, where we were bombarded with offers of taxis. Phlopp had given me the name of a hotel to stay in that he recommended, but Nancy having recently travelled here with Adrian, said that we would try the hotel she had stayed in first. They were both in the same area. We were in walking distance of the hotels from the station, but because of Nancy's baggage we took a taxi. The hotel was down a dingy back street, and as we entered the lobby, which contained just a desk, we asked the man behind it if they had a double room for a week. They did. A rather portly porter was summoned to help take our bags up the three flights of dark stairs to our room. He followed us upstairs, huffing and puffing behind us, and directing us as to which way to go. The room was small, dark, and cheerless, but it had an en suite bathroom and the bedding was clean. It was cheap, albeit not so cheerful. A notice told us that there was no running hot water, but that the management would be delighted to deliver this at the guest's request. I was surprised that the porter was not a tad slimmer with all the running up and down stairs that he did.

Nestled Amongst Temples

To my surprise, I found that I liked Delhi. I had imagined it to be of a similar ilk to Mumbai, busy, bustling, and dirty, but it was much more relaxed and seemed to have more space and green areas. There were cows wandering around the city too, which I had not witnessed in Mumbai as it was too congested with roads and traffic. There were plenty of rooftop restaurants in the area where we were located, and these were something I had not experienced before in India. We would walk up four or five flights of stairs to be bombarded with panoramic views over the area, whilst we ate brunch or dinner.

Our hotel was situated off a main road, which was a busy shopping area, and so Nancy and I took full advantage of this to shop for presents. I bought carved wooden boxes, silk scarves, notebooks of hand pressed paper, pens that were encrusted with tiny diamond shaped mirrors, jewelled trinket boxes, and lots of Indian clothes. My daughters and I were fond of the baggy Indian trousers in cotton, which were so comfy for lounging around the house and so cheap to buy here. I bought several pairs of these to distribute to friends and family back at home. I also bought lots of children's clothes for Otis, little Indian shirts which were collarless and pulled over his head and mini versions of the baggy trousers. They had little suits for children with matching baggy trousers and shirts and I bought several of these. We were going past a shop one day, when I saw the most elaborate little suit. It was in gold cloth and consisted of loose drawstring waist trousers, a little shirt with a mandarin collar that was encrusted in gold gems, a cummerbund with tassels, and a long matching waistcoat that went down to the knee, which was also encrusted with gold jewels and embroidery. It was simply gorgeous and so striking. I could just imagine Otis wearing this, with his black curly hair setting off the little antique gold outfit superbly.

"When's he going to wear that?" Nancy had asked sensibly.

"I don't know, maybe to a party of something, but it's so cute and I can just see him in it, looking gorgeous." So I bought the totally impractical little suit, despite it being quite pricey. As it happened, he did wear it later that year for a rather special, unexpected, family occasion.

*

Nancy and I became quite close again during our two weeks of travelling, and all the tension and discord of the previous months dissipated.

"You're an easy travel companion, aren't you, Mama," Nancy had informed me one morning, when she had asked me what I wanted to do that day and I had assured her that I was happy to fit in with whatever her plans were. Nancy had a travel book with her and so we looked up places to visit in the area. There was a Sikh temple quite nearby that was renowned for its architecture, having a gilded roof and equally magnificent interior. We visited and it appeared to be some sort of feast day or celebration when we arrived, as there were queues of people waiting to enter and a service being held inside. We covered our heads with our dupattas, removed our shoes, and entered the magnificent building. Everywhere was gilt and marble and it was reminiscent of the style of Marseilles. A bearded priest was conducting the service, but people were wandering around the building nonetheless. A large, gilded, coffin like structure, protected by a glass case, lay on a stand in one corner of the building, but there was no guide to instruct us as to what the artefacts were, so we were left to guess. Outside was a large, square, man-made lake that contained numerous large carp, and people were bathing and paddling in this, as the fish swam around them. We took photographs outside of the building, looking quite native with our headscarves and brown skin.

Another temple that we visited, a train ride away from Delhi, was the more modern Lotus Temple. It was made out of white marble and shaped like a huge lotus flower. It was simply beautiful. Inside it was spacious and airy with plain wooden benches and no adornments, the intricate structure of the white marble speaking for itself. It was an interdenominational temple and there were collection boxes asking for donations towards its upkeep. Nancy and I stayed in the temple for around an hour, sitting on the benches in quiet reflection. It was a space that lent itself perfectly to prayer and contemplation.

I did not see poverty in Delhi to the same scale that I had witnessed it in Mumbai; there were no families camping out on the streets and although people begged, it did not appear to be in the same numbers. I did meet one beggar though, who remained in my memory. He was a young boy, who looked around nine or ten years of age, although he could have been older. He had a bent foot, which he dragged slightly and he was barefoot, dressed in tatty, dirty clothes. He looked unkempt and unwashed. He approached me asking for money and when I got out my purse to give him some rupees, he asked me if I would follow him, as he wanted to show me something. It was not far, he assured me. I looked at Nancy and she shrugged. We were both puzzled that he had not taken the money, but as we were on a busy main road, we were not too concerned about following him. "What are you showing us," I asked.

"Please, madam, we are nearly there," he said then proceeded to tell me that he was an orphan who had a young baby sister to care for. I sympathised with his plight and again offered to give his some rupees, but he refused, still insisting that I follow him. He then stopped outside a street stall, where he told us that he wanted to buy some baby milk for his young sister and would I please pay for this. Unfortunately for the young man and shopkeeper, I had read about this scam, whereby the tourist pays an extortionate amount for the baby milk, which is then returned to the shopkeeper with a payment given to the beggar concerned. I refused to buy the milk, but gave the boy 20 rupees and told him to buy himself some food. I had heard of Fagan type characters in Indian cities who had squads of beggar children working for them, and I suspected that the boy might be one of these. It was a sad affair and left Nancy and I quite upset afterwards.

*

When booking the train tickets in Anjuna, I had only been able to book tickets into Delhi, but not out of the city. I was informed that there was only a limited ticket allocation for agents, but that I should be able to buy outbound tickets at Delhi, which was a major station. Nancy and I had decided to travel to Pushkar, which was a small town that many of the market traders visited to buy stock. It had numerous clothes and jewellery manufacturers, so ready-made goods could be bought cheaply at wholesale prices and, also, original designs could be made up to order. Nancy had visited the area on her previous trip with Adrian, and had already sourced manufacturers to work with her designs, for her next range of MamaNoo clothes and jewellery. We intended staying in Pushkar for one week and then travelling to Mumbai from where we were both flying home, Nancy ten days later than me.

We went along to Delhi station to buy our train tickets to Ajmer, the nearest station to Pushkar and from there on to Mumbai. The queue at the train station for tickets was never ending, and we waited in line for around two hours, only to be told at the end of this that there were no tickets available. The clerk, helpfully, informed us though, that there were a number of tickets reserved for tourists and to try the tourist office, situated on the first floor. We went along to the tourist office where inside there was a waiting area and signs instructing tourists to complete the forms provided with destination and informing that passports or copies of these were required. We did not have our passports with us but we queued anyway to ask if there were tickets available for our destinations, to be informed that there were, and the clerk helpfully told us he could reserve two for us, if we paid now and returned later with our passports or copies. We completed the forms for two, second-class sleeper tickets, signed that we were tourists, paid the clerk and he put our tickets in a drawer for us to collect the following day with our passport evidence, as agreed.

"This is going to be a bit tricky," Nancy informed me, as we were leaving the building.

"Why what's the matter?" I asked confused.

"I'm not a tourist, Mum, I'm still out here on my visa from work."

I had forgotten all about Nancy's visa. Her boss, from the company she had worked for in Mumbai, had agreed to extend her visa for six months if she worked an extra three weeks, in order to get ready for a show in Paris that they were exhibiting at. This was way back in October and, at the time, had saved Nancy a lot of hassle with reapplying for visas.

"Well, you're still a tourist aren't you?" I asked. "Well, you're not Indian."

"No, it specifically stated that you had to be travelling on a tourist visa."

"Do you think we can sweet talk him tomorrow, or cry, or something?"

"I don't think it will do any good, Mama. You know what they are like for officialdom."

"We're stuffed then. What are we going to do?"

"Forge a copy of my passport." Nancy replied.

"That's a bit drastic, darling. How do you intend to do that?

"I'll show you."

And she did just that. She studied the visa on my passport and then in the same typeface and font size as her own visa, typed a document on her laptop, the same entry and exit dates as my visa and the words "tourist visa." She then put these onto a memory stick and went along to a stationery shop where she photocopied her passport; printed off the document she had typed, and bought some tipex, paper glue, and a craft knife. On return from the shop, she carefully cut out the printed words and dates with the knife and stuck these over the relevant bits on the photocopy of her visa.

"What's the tippex for?" I asked puzzled.

"Wait and see." she answered.

"Where did you learn to do this?" I asked, concerned.

"When I used to design cards, covering up errors and things." She answered, to my obvious relief.

On return from photocopying the first cut and paste photocopy of her visa, she carefully tipexed the new copy, as the edges of the paper that she had glued on, could still be faintly seen.

"Now we can photocopy this again in the morning before we go to the station. I don't want to go back photocopying again now, in case they get suspicious." She said; I felt like a bank forger.

In the morning Nancy photocopied the visa copy again and it looked authentic, but we were still nervous on our way back to the station. "Do you want me to do it?" I asked, "And then if he notices anything dodgy, I can say I don't know anything about it, as it's not my passport."

"No, I'll do it." Nancy said.

I felt so nervous that I could not wait in the room and wandered around the station for around 20 minutes, until my phone rang and it was Nancy on the other end.

"How did it go?" I asked apprehensively.

"Great" she replied, "I've got the tickets."

"Oh, well done, darling."

We met up and went for coffee, whereby she laughingly informed me that she had panicked at the last moment, and fearing police involvement if she was caught, had just handed over her actual passport that was in her handbag. The same clerk as the previous day opened the passport at the visa page, carefully copied down the number and exit date and then handed it back to her with the tickets. He had not even noticed that it was a work visa. After all that effort and angst!

Chapter 22: Pushkar

Once again, we arrived at Delhi train station and lugged my suitcase and Nancy's numerous bags to the platform. The journey to Ajmer was around six hours long and quite uneventful, apart from the difference between first and second-class travel. The carriages for this journey were old and tatty, being painted a rust coloured red that was faded and dirty. The windows did not contain glass, but had bars instead like a jail cell. There were six bunks per carriage, three on either side and during our journey, being in daylight, the second bunk was placed flat against the wall, becoming the back cushioning for the seats, which was the bottom bunk. There was no food on this journey, but when the train stopped at stations, hawkers would come to the windows selling hot food and fruit through the bars.

The gypsies, Nancy had bemoaned missing when travelling by first-class, boarded the second-class carriages of this train. They announced their arrival by banging their drums and shouting, "Hoy! Hoy!" They then proceeded to go from carriage to carriage, singing loudly and banging their drums in accompaniment. They were entertaining and we enjoyed the show, tipping them well in appreciation. Then they stepped off the train at the next station and boarded another one, to entertain those passengers in the same fashion. We were also visited in the second-class carriages by hijras, who we were familiar with from their visits to the markets. These transvestite (sometimes eunuch) men would dress in gaudy female clothes, wearing heavy make-up, in a way that did nothing to disguise the fact that they were not really women. It was obviously their intent to be identified as hijras. The majority of Indian people seemed nervous whenever they appeared and would pay them money to go away or, otherwise, the hijras would curse them. They arrived on our carriage with their exaggerated female gestures, hands on hips and flinging their hands out shouting in falsetto voices, "Rupees, rupees." Nancy and I had just spent the last of our small rupee notes buying samosas and water at the last station and had only large notes left. As one of them came over demanding money, we apologised and explained that we had no money to give them. He snarled at us in broken English, "Pay rupee or I give curse!"

"You can curse all you want to," I informed him, "but we've no rupees to give you." His face screwed up with anger, when Nancy, looking at his hand which he still had on his hip, suddenly piped up,

"Ooh, I like your ring. Look at his ring, Mama, isn't it beautiful." It was a large, golden paste ring depicting a lotus flower: she would have scorned it had she spotted it in other circumstances.

He suddenly broke out laughing at her outburst and wiggled the fingers of his ringed hand at her. "No money, no pay," he announced still smiling at us and waving goodbye to us dramatically, he flounced out of the carriage. We too burst into laughter.

*

Nestled Amongst Temples

Pushkar was a bustling little town with a huge lake, regarded as holy, situated at the side of a very old temple. It was in the middle of a rural area and was flanked with factories on the outskirts. It was popular with visitors on account of the holy lake and seemed to be part of the tourist trail. Rajistan was, yet again, different to the other states I had visited and another testament to India's diversity. Here the men wore enormous turbans, far larger than anywhere else I had seen in India and it was not only Sikh men who wore them, but most of the local men. The turbans were of bright colours too, some day-glow orange or acid yellow and, likewise, the women wore bright saris of contrasting hues; pink, orange and greens being favoured colours. Pushkar, I discovered was a riot of colour.

We stayed in a lovely little guesthouse that Nancy had stayed at a few weeks previously. It was surrounded by a wall and was accessed by a high, arched gateway. Inside the courtyard was a large house, a temple, beautiful gardens, and a row of single storey villas, one of which we booked into. The owner was delighted to see Nancy again and welcomed her back, shaking hands with us both, beaming. Nancy introduced me as her mother and he was thrilled that she had returned so soon and with her mother in tow. He obviously took this as a huge compliment. He showed us to our room, which was a little row of stone built villas, at the side of a beautiful garden, and consisted of a bedroom and bathroom. We unloaded our bags and without getting changed, went out for dinner.

Pushkar, like Delhi, favoured roof top restaurants and Nancy took me to one of her favourites, The Babas, discovered during her last visit. We ate a delicious Indian meal that was incredibly cheap compared to Goa and Delhi prices, and then Nancy introduced me to "Say Hello To The Queen," which became a firm favourite of ours during our time in Pushkar. This was a dessert devised, supposedly, when the British ruled in India, and consisted of crushed biscuits, hot chocolate sauce, bananas, ice cream, and sometimes fresh cream and meringue, depending on where it was served. It was delicious and certainly a make-yourself-sick dish. In Pushkar, we made sure that there was always time for chai and room for "Say Hello To The Queen." We had a lovely week, visiting the lake and dining out at different restaurants in the evenings, whilst fitting in visits to factories and ordering and waiting for Nancy's designs of cardigans, scarves, and jewellery to be made.

The main house where our villa was situated had a small outhouse that was fitted as a kitchen, and a cook was stationed there to cater for the guests. All week, we ordered our breakfasts off him and sometimes lunch too, as the food was cheap and tasty. He was very knowledgeable about Indian history and familiar with the Rajistan region and when he brought the food over to us, as we sat outside our little room, he would always sit down for a few minutes and chat to us. His English was very good and his wisdom, insights, and knowledge of India inspiring. The first time we breakfasted, he asked us to write down what we had ordered, and told us that he would bill us at the end of the week. On our last day, he arrived with our breakfasts, the order sheets on which we had written down our food, and a menu with prices, requesting, politely, that we total our bill. I presumed that this was his nice way of asking us to pay and a demonstration of his honesty; in my mind, he had already totted up the bill and knew exactly how much we owed. So I added it all up and went to the little kitchen to pay. As I handed over the money, I added,

"I think I've calculated it all correctly, is that right?"

He half smiled at me, looking embarrassed and replied, "Apologies, madam, but I cannot check as I cannot read. That is why I burdened you to total it for me." It was a sad realisation on my part.

The other staff at the guesthouse were lovely and friendly with us too, always waving and stopping to chat. As we crossed the garden to the gateway, there were often women sitting on the steps outside of the entrance to the temple. I was not sure if they belonged to the house that rented out the rooms, or if they were visitors to the temple, but they were always friendly with us, shouting out "hello," and waving as we walked past. One day, as we walked into the courtyard, the women called us over and pointed to the anklets that we wore, shaking their heads. We were confused and asked them what they meant, and in sign language they shook their heads and pointed to their own anklets on both ankles, clearly indicating that it was incorrect to wear anklets on one leg only. Then they laughingly pointed to Nancy's nose piercing, which was in her left nostril, and shook their heads again, pointing to their own nose rings, which were in their right nostrils. The inference was clear, we did not have a clue what we were doing when it came to anklets and nose rings. Nancy shrugged, what could she say in the face of their obvious superior knowledge of these things, and we laughed with them sharing the cultural joke.

Not every interchange in Pushkar was so innocent, unfortunately. Whilst walking through the small town we were accosted by men requesting that they show us the holy lake, which would not cost us any money they informed us. Nancy had warned me about them, telling me that when she had visited previously, she went with one of the men and a few other tourists to see the lake. He and an accomplice had shown them all around, including the temple, and then asked them to pray with him, whilst still inside the temple. He said a prayer and they had to repeat it after him. It went along the following lines:

I promise to the gods that I will live a good life.

I promise to the gods that I will help others.

I promise to the gods that I will not lie or steal.

I promise to the gods that I will not do bad things.

I promise to the gods that I will support them financially.

I promise to the gods that I will be a good person.

The men then asked for 5,000 rupees each from the tourists in support of the temple. When people refused, the men, acting aghast, said that they had just promised the gods to assist financially and they could not renege on this. Nancy said that one of the men was posted at the closed temple door blocking the exit. Some of the tourists handed over the money and were let out. Nancy insisted that she did not have the money and started to repeat loudly that they had to let her out. They did in the end move away from the door, but only after she had promised to go to the ATM and withdraw the cash and return, which, of course, she had no intention of doing. She said that it was a scary experience though. This time around, whenever they approached us, Nancy made a point of telling any visitors in the vicinity not to accompany them, as it was a scam. The men soon learnt to avoid us after the first couple of days.

Also, on Nancy's previous visit to Pushkar, she had gone to see a few of the factories to find out if any of them could make up her designs and to see how long this would take. She had found one factory that she had struck up a good relationship with the owner and he assured her that he could make small numbers of her garments in a few days. She had brought back samples of materials and edgings in order to choose her designs. The second day in Pushkar, we visited the factory on the outskirts of the town and Nancy took in her designs and swatch samples. We had saved enough money to have 30 cardigans and 30 large scarves made up to Nancy's designs in a choice of colour-ways. Nancy discussed this with the factory owner, who was friendly and obliging, writing down her request in his little notebook. He informed us that the garments would be ready in three days. He had already made up a sample of both a cardigan and scarf at her last visit and she was happy with the quality of these. She had previously negotiated prices with him and she discussed this with him again now, reaffirming the prices. I was beginning to discover that my daughter was quite an accomplished businesswoman, having no problems with negotiating fair deals with experienced businessmen and holding her own successfully. I felt quite in awe of her as she haggled on prices with no sign of difficulty or embarrassment.

When we returned to the factory a few days later to collect the goods, the order was not quite completed, we were told, and the owner suggested that we wait whilst it was finished. We waited a while and then walked downstairs to the small factory floor where the workers were just commencing to make our order. Nancy was furious and tackled the manager, he confessed he had been very busy, but that he would put all of his staff on completing our order now. Two hours later and it was finished, but the order was not as Nancy had requested, with many of the garments made from different materials and trimmings. Nancy sorted through all of the order and removed the ones she did not want. The manager said that he had run out of some of the material she had requested, but that he could make more of certain colour-ways. Nancy refused his offer and renegotiated the price, letting her displeasure be felt. He had sewn onto the clothes the black and gold MamaNoo labels that Nancy had ordered in Mumbai, several months ago. They looked lovely and I felt proud to see the labels attached to the clothes, despite the problems we had encountered with the order. The owner offered to take us back to the guesthouse on his motorbike, taking one of us and then coming back for the other, as he did not have his car with him that day. I declined, as I was nervous riding pillion on motorbikes without a helmet, especially seeing the speed and road sense in India. So we shook hands and I walked back whilst Nancy rode pillion on the back of the motorbike with a huge bundle of clothes perched on her lap. Only in India, I thought, where it is not uncommon to see a family of four on one scooter.

We spent the last couple of days in Pushkar parcelling up the MamaNoo stock and sending this back to England, where Nancy intended setting up an internet shop. Her dream was to have a little boutique in a trendy area which she would fill with her own designs of stationery, artworks, clothing, and jewellery, but this was a long way off yet. As there was no wrapping service in

Pushkar we came up with the idea of covering the boxes in clingfilm, which would work in the same way as the material wrapping we had used in Goa. We trailed around the town asking in every grocery store, but nobody sold this. Eventually as a last resort we asked at a hardware store, where a friendly young assistant told us that he thought they might have a roll in the back that was part used. He talked to the shop owner who obviously noted that we were tourists and thought rupees. The owner, who spoke no English, and used the young assistant as a translator, went into the back and came out with a roll of dusty clingfilm. As it was better than nothing, we asked how much it would cost. Unsmiling and officious, he dusted down the roll and then placed this on his weighing scales, jotting down calculations on a pad. Nancy and I tried not to laugh. We stopped smiling when he told us the price.

"Let's just leave it," I said, fed up with people charging us ridiculous prices because we were tourists.

"It's better than nothing, Mama," Nancy reasoned. "If the boxes break we will have lost a lot more than this."

So we paid the extortionate price whilst the young assistant, looking totally embarrassed, whispered to us surreptitiously, "I am so sorry, madams." We managed to wrap two of the boxes with the roll, using realms of sellotape to wrap the other two. They all arrived safely back in England. Since then, I always think of that dusty, dark little shop every time I use clingfilm.

*

I was sorry to be leaving Pushkar, not only because I liked the little town, but also because it marked the end of my extended stay in India. We once again packed our numerous bags and took a taxi to the station a half hour ride away. The journey to Mumbai was another overnight one and I was booked onto the middle bunk and Nancy the top bunk of the carriage. I soon discovered that she had the best seat by far, as she could retire to lay prone whenever she chose, whereas I had to wait until the person on the bottom bunk wished to lie down, before I could pull up my bunk and fasten it with chains to the bunk above.

We passed the time, as on previous journeys, by reading, listening to music, sometimes chatting, and, of course, eating. Meals were included on this trip and we, once again, looked forward to the break from the monotony of travel that these provided. Whist eating one meal, something dropped from the bunk above onto my lap next to the vegetable curry and I was horrified to find it was a small cockroach. I let out a cry and instinctively flicked it off me, only to send it flying into the lap of the gentleman sat in the opposite seat. He looked down at his leg calmly, then flicked it onto the floor and crushed it with his foot. I was really enjoying my meal up until that point. It also put me off longing for bedtime as I imagined sleeping whilst those creatures crawled over me. Horrid.

We stopped at a station on route and in the doorway of a stopped train on another track was a man we presumed to be a Baba. He had a long beard and wore coral coloured robes. On his head was an enormous hat, which was also coral coloured and looked like a fat version of a chef's hat. He saw Nancy and I looking over at him and beamed at us. He was smoking a cigarette and, as quite often Babas smoke chillums, large pipes containing hashish, I imitated the smoking of a chillum, which is done by placing the chillum pipe above the head with one hand and sucking from underneath with the head tilted. Not easy to mistake what I was miming. He laughed at me. I got out my camera and took his photograph. Then he stepped off the train and started to walk across the tracks towards us. "Oh no," Nancy said. "He's coming begging." As he approached the window, I showed him the camera with his photo in the screen. He smiled and put his closed hand through the bars saying, "I have a gift for you." He put something small into my hand and then turned and walked back to his train. It was a lump of hashish. "How wrong were we?" I said to Nancy. "He wanted to give to us, not to take." We enthusiastically waved goodbye as our train pulled out of the station.

Eventually the lady on the bottom bunk decided that she wanted to lie down and I was able to lift up my bunk and fasten it to Nancy's bunk above mine with the chains provided for this purpose. I lay down and covered myself with my dupatta, but I could not sleep. Cockroaches invaded my thoughts, and as it darkened outside and there were no lights, it became worse. I started to imagine them crawling over me. I suddenly remembered the Baba's gift and knew from my student days that hashish made me sleepy, especially when eaten. I put my hand into my pocket and pulled out the lump and bit it in half, chewing it slowly. I lay awake for quite a while and then suddenly found myself chuckling and thinking that I had shared my bed with far worse creatures than cockroaches in my time. The gift was

257

beginning to work its magic. I woke up in the morning after a good night sleep of the most vivid dreams. I felt a little groggy, but otherwise happy and relaxed. Thank you, Baba.

On the way into Mumbai the train passed by the side of the Dharavi slums, where shacks of houses spread for miles. Unclothed children waved at us as we sped past and families sat cooking at the side of the tracks or tended to their ablutions. It seemed to be life at its most raw and naked.

*

Nancy and I had discussed what we were going to do when we arrived in Mumbai, as my plane was not leaving until late that evening. Nancy was staying with a friend who we were meeting later that day. We had decided to go straight to one of the hotels Nancy knew, which was next to the sea, and pay for a day pass whereby we could spend the day swimming in their pool and drinking cocktails. We could use their showers and get changed here too, ready for meeting Clarissa in the early evening. So that is exactly what we did. We had a lovely restful day, sunbathing and swimming in the pool and then ate lunch, which was a lot pricier than in Pushkar and certainly not as tasty.

Clarissa and her boyfriend lived in Mumbai, not far from the hotel, and they employed a chauffeur to drive them around in the crazy Mumbai traffic. She picked us up at the hotel, in her chauffeured car and we discussed what restaurant we wanted to eat at. Firstly though, Clarissa asked her driver to take us to a bar as she wanted to watch an English football match that was playing; although American, she followed an English football team. I discovered to my horror that both Clarissa and her driver had a death wish. He drove like a maniac in the already crazy traffic of Mumbai and Clarissa, laughingly, egged him on. Even Nancy, who was very used to the city and driving in this traffic, admitted that his driving unnerved her. I arrived at the bar and ordered a strong drink. Clarissa, oblivious to my distress, chatted away happily whilst keeping one eye on the football match on screen. She asked us how the journey had been and we told her the tale of the Baba. I also recounted my good night sleep and confessed the remedy for this. Clarissa and Nancy both wanted to try it and asked did I still have the other piece. So we bit the little chunk into three and each nibbled a crumb. It was not much, but it ensured that we had a rather frivolous and fun filled evening. We dined at a lovely traditional Indian restaurant and then went back to Clarissa's apartment for coffee. Clarissa had kindly arranged for her chauffeur to drive me to the airport although I earnestly tried to resist, but she would not hear of this. It was the ride from Hell and certainly removed any apprehension about my imminent flying. Although he was reluctant to take it, I tipped him when I got out of the car; not in gratitude for his driving, but because I was so relieved to have made it to the airport alive. I certainly left India in a memorable whirl!

Epilogue

Once Phlopp had left Goa to go travelling, the texts and phone calls between us became fewer and fewer and with a change of tone on his part, I noticed. Instead of *"mon cherie"* I had become *"mon amie"* and there was no more mention of meeting up in Delhi before he left for France. Neither had there been any discussions before we parted of meeting up at a later date in France or England and I suddenly realised how strange and unfinished this all was; I also realised that he had not given me his phone number in France, I didn't know his Skype address and my only way of contacting him was via email. As I was busy travelling with Nancy the last few weeks in India the matter became shelved to some degree. I mentioned it to Nancy and we decided he was probably busy sketching his deities in temples and preparing for going back to France; he would be winding down, much as we were and probably saw little point in constantly texting and phoning me. It was strange though and not in keeping with his previous affectionate behaviour.

I flew back to England a few weeks before Nancy and had a couple of weeks at home before I returned to work after my six month break. I caught up with my family, had my gorgeous grandson to stay with me, who had grown so much, and generally had time to wind down after my adventures and think. After I was home in

England for a few days, it suddenly dawned on me why I had not heard from Phlopp and why he had cooled off so noticeably in the last few weeks, of course, it was obvious. The man was married! It all fitted perfectly. The phone calls from his mother, where he would walk away to answer them. Not arranging to meet up once we were back home in our respective countries. Insisting that I come back next season to be with him. When I asked him about his apartment in France he told me that he had sublet it for the four months he was away, which now, with hindsight, seemed improbable. Not providing me with his phone number or Skype address, but only an email contact; it was all so obvious. I was shocked though, still not wanting to believe what was staring me in the face. He was so spiritual, so genuine.

I searched his name online and found pictures of him at an art exhibition in Goa a couple of years earlier, with his arm around a female, not too unlike myself in looks. I found a website where he sold his paintings which included a short biography of the artist and his studio was not where he had told me, he must have lied in case I turned up to look for him. Shock turned to anger and I emailed him accusing him of lying and being married. Two weeks later he replied saying he was not and had never been married. Even now he could not tell the truth. The old adage that liars need good memories rang true as he had already told me on several occasions that he had been married. According to his previous tales, his wife and he had divorced because he did not earn enough money. He had told me that she worked as a curator in a museum; so she would be unable to accompany him to India for the four month holidays that Phlopp enjoyed as a freelance artist. All the pieces fitted.

He emailed me a few more times after this, with chatty emails about his paintings, but I just could not bring myself to reply. I was too hurt. In the cold light of day, when it was all less raw and painful, I wondered if I would still have embarked on the relationship with him had he told me when we first met that he was married. I really did not have an answer, but it was not an immediate "no" that sprang to mind. Somehow there was comfort in this as it gave me back some control. I felt duped, stupid, and naïve on top of everything else.

So at the end of my six months of travel what had I learnt, what had I gained, and what had I lost? It was an experience that I will never forget although I do not necessarily want to repeat it. I learnt that I can cope quite well in a strange country with different customs and cultures and make my way quite easily. I gained confidence in this respect and could now, quite happily, holiday abroad on my own should I desire to. This is a big step for me. I learnt about the kindness of strangers and how people we trust are not necessarily all they appear to be. I realised how important my family are and how much I miss them when I am not near to them. I realised that life is for living, and a step away from the daily grind is refreshing for the soul. I would recommend this as a cure for a lacklustre life, it puts things in perspective, shakes it all up a little. I realised how lucky I am, and how lucky all of us living in developed countries are in terms of healthcare and education, which we often take for granted and even moan about. I learnt that I can't escape from myself no matter how far I travel, it's still the same me and the same joys and problems appear because of this.

So did India's spirituality rub off on me as I imagined before my travels? Perhaps. These days I am more aware of the spirituality that I am surrounded by, and how my behaviours have impact on others far beyond the reach I imagine. There is no escaping this. Like the announcement at Margoa station when Nancy and I were waiting for the Delhi train to arrive:

"This is an announcement from Indian Railways. Have you bought your train ticket? It is a crime to travel on Indian Railways without a train ticket. You will be prosecuted if you are caught travelling on the trains without a ticket. Remember, Lord Ganesh can see you and he knows if you have bought your ticket. You may cheat Indian Railways, but you cannot cheat Lord Ganesh."

About the Author

Jillain McKay lives in Manchester in the United Kingdom. She holds a Doctorate in Education and works full-time as a senior lecturer at the University of Manchester having been employed in academia for over twenty years.

Although born and brought up in the northwest of England, she has also lived in New York City and spent six months travelling in India which became the basis for her first novel Nestled Amongst Temples.

Jill has written numerous academic publications, but this is her first venture into writing for an audience outside of education.

Jill can be contacted via her Facebook page: Jillain McKay and Twitter account @jillainmckay

www.tri-pub.com

Printed in Great Britain
by Amazon.co.uk, Ltd.,
Marston Gate.